mental traveler

mental traveler

A Father, a Son, and a
Journey through Schizophrenia

w.j.t. mitchell

The University of Chicago Press · Chicago and London

The University of Chicago Press, Chicago 60637
The University of Chicago Press, Ltd., London
© 2020 by The University of Chicago
Published 2020
Printed in the United States of America

29 28 27 26 25 24 23 22 21 20   1 2 3 4 5

ISBN-13: 978-0-226-69593-8 (cloth)
ISBN-13: 978-0-226-69609-6 (e-book)
DOI: https://doi.org/10.7208/chicago/9780226696096.001.0001

Library of Congress Cataloging-in-Publication Data

Names: Mitchell, W. J. T. (William John Thomas), 1942– author. | Misurell-Mitchell,
Janice.
Title: Mental traveler : a father, a son, and a journey through schizophrenia /
W. J. T. Mitchell.
Description: Chicago ; London : The University of Chicago Press, 2020.
Identifiers: LCCN 2019052214 | ISBN 9780226695938 (cloth) | ISBN 9780226696096
(ebook)
Subjects: LCSH: Mitchell, Gabriel, 1973-2012. | Mitchell, Gabriel, 1973–2012—
Mental health. | Mitchell, W. J. T. (William John Thomas), 1942– —Family. |
Schizophrenics—Illinois—Chicago—Biography. | Artists—Illinois—Chicago—
Biography. | Motion picture producers and directors—Illinois—Chicago—
Biography. | Mentally ill—Family relationships. | Fathers and sons. | Art and
mental illness. | Mental illness in motion pictures. | LCGFT: Biographies.
Classification: LCC RC514 .M526 2020 | DDC 616.89/80092 [B]—dc23
LC record available at https://lccn.loc.gov/2019052214

♾ This paper meets the requirements of ANSI/NISO Z39.48-1992
(Permanence of Paper).

I travelled through a land of men
A land of men and women too
And heard and saw such dreadful things
As cold earth wanderers never knew.

WILLIAM BLAKE, "The Mental Traveller"

CONTENTS

PREFACE

There are two kinds of books: the ones you want to write, and the ones you have to write. I have written quite a few of the first kind, but this is not one of them. It is a memoir of the life and death of my son, Gabriel Mitchell, who struggled with schizophrenia for twenty years until his suicide at age thirty-eight. It is not a book I wanted to write, or ever expected that I would write, until the fatal day of June 24, 2012.

In many ways, Gabe was a typical case of schizophrenia. First onset of symptoms—depression, anger, delusions, hallucinations—around age nineteen. Dropping out of college and into the mental health system, hospitalization, medications, therapies, halfway houses. A decade spent battling addiction to alcohol and drugs, and enduring the stigma that comes with a diagnosis of schizophrenia. Part-time employment as a grocery clerk. An early death at thirty-eight, probably triggered by overwork and the stress of passing for "healthy" and "normal." End of story.

But as anyone who has lived with mental illness knows, typical cases are also deeply singular and individual. Everyone goes crazy in their own way, and every family has its own way of dealing with their disturbed son or daughter, brother or sister, father or mother. Every derangement is a response to an arrangement, a de-arrangement of social and institutional circumstances. Although mental illness often results in isolation from family and society, it never happens alone. Some families are shattered; some become stronger. Some victims surrender and disappear into their symptoms, living out their days in quiet suffering. Others fight back with every means at their disposal. This is the story of someone who fought back and attempted to see his own madness with complete lucidity, and to see through it to something beyond. It is also the story of a family that helped him survive schizophrenia for twenty years and is now determined that his life will endure beyond his suicide. As Gabe once put it, "People are always changing. Even beyond the grave, they are changing."

I have tried to see *through* Gabe's madness, to see beyond the medical labels and stereotypes and apprehend the concrete individual who himself attempted to look back at madness from the inside with art and work and skill. Of course, I think my son was very special, and I know that I share this view with every parent who has lost a child. But specialness is both typical and specific, ordinary and singular. My aim here is to specify and commemorate the unrepeatable life of my son, to tell the story of his struggle and to make you see him clearly right up to the moment of his departure and beyond. If this story helps others who are blessed with a beloved "mental traveler," so much the better.

To call someone "a schizophrenic," as if it named an identity rather than an illness, is without question politically incorrect. Better to say "a person with schizophrenia," or (following R. D. Laing) "a so-called schizophrenic." Laing's formulation has the advantage of recognizing that schizophrenia, like diabetes, is an illness that *becomes* an identity—what society calls you whether you like it or not. It is not a chosen identity but is imposed from outside, most fatefully by medical authorities. For oneself, the choice is between saying "I *have* schizophrenia," or "I *am* a schizophrenic." Gabe was comfortable saying either, choosing the identity label when he was feeling militantly political about affirming schizophrenia as a minority position. I have tried not to fuss over these distinctions very much in these pages. When I apply the word "schizophrenic" to a person, you should read it as silently adding "so-called" to recognize that it is a label applied from without, rarely from within.

CHAPTER ONE

"I Need to Become Homeless"

In the fall of 1991 I received an urgent phone message from Gabe, just a few weeks after he enrolled as a freshman at NYU. He had something important to tell me, and I must call back immediately. What could it be? Some insight into his choice of a major? Has he met the girl of his dreams? All our phone conversations to that point had been filled with enthusiasm. He loved his classes, especially philosophy. "All my teachers love me, especially Dr. F, who thinks I'm brilliant." The student parties and the café scene of Greenwich Village were "beyond cool." I flashed back to my own experiences as a college freshman in 1960, on my own for the first time, discovering sex and existentialism. Although we had thought a small rural liberal arts college might have been a better place for Gabe, he was enthralled with the idea of New York. And indeed, it seemed the perfect place for his boundless curiosity and off-beat sensibilities. Gabe had always been a seeker, and it was not unusual for him to announce a new passion that would mark a turning point in his life.

When I made the call, he got right to the point. "Dad, I have discovered the authentic way of life. It's obvious to me that I have to give up everything and become homeless." "Well, that's really interesting," I said, warily putting on my college counselor hat. "I'm sure that NYU has great programs in social work that would be just the thing if you want to work with the homeless." "No, Dad. I don't want to *work* with the homeless. I need to *become* homeless. You and Mom are completely clueless about what life really is. You live in an illusion of comfort, surrounded by your books and records and your warm house. The homeless are the only people I've met here who are in touch with reality." Then I tried the old "reality principle" gambit. "Yes," I said. "They are in touch with reality, but it is a terrible reality, filled with suffering. They go hungry. They sleep on park benches." He was ready for that. "What do you really know about it? Have you talked to homeless people? Hung out with them? You are the one who is refusing to see the reality."

It wasn't the first or last time Gabe told me how clueless his mother and I were. Gabe had spent his high school years roaming Chicago with his graffiti gang, skateboarding, and partying. I knew that he had seen aspects of life in the city that were terra incognita to me in my cloistered academic life, or to my wife, Janice, a composer and performer in the city's avant-garde music scene. But becoming homeless? This was a new twist in his quest for reality.

The next shoe dropped when he told me that he needed an advance on his allowance because he had given most of his book money to the panhandlers in Washington Square.

When they would ask him for help to get something to eat, he would take them to lunch. When they told him they had no place to sleep, he tried to smuggle them into the dorm. "But the people at the dorm don't like it much. They say it's against some policy, which is ridiculous, because it's my room, and you're paying for it. I have a right to bring my friends there."

When he told me that he had given away his winter coat to a homeless man, I decided to keep him on the phone as long as possible, first by changing the subject to sports. We plunged into a discussion of the exploits of Michael Jordan and the Chicago Bulls, and the possibility of catching a game together during Christmas vacation.

Which led naturally to "Speaking of Christmas, Dad. Do you suppose I could ask Santa for a new CD player?" "Absolutely," I said. I can still feel my sigh of relief at this return to materialism and normality. I suppressed the urge to ask him where he was going to plug it in when he was sleeping on a park bench.

What I did not know at the time was that Gabe was falling into a mental illness that would, after a twenty-year struggle, cause him to end his life. This is the story of those decades, a time in which he fought his way through both the symptoms and the diagnosis of schizophrenia, and navigated the labyrinth of the mental health system to achieve a measure of stability and an outpouring of creativity. In the final years of his life, he began to turn his artistic talents to the subject of mental illness itself, with the aim of producing a cinematic *histoire de la folie* modeled on Jean-Luc Godard's *Histoire du cinéma*. In the winter of 2011, he made a ten-minute pilot for this film entitled *Crazy Talk*. His aims were clear: "I want to put my illness to work," he said. "My goal is to transform schizophrenia from a death sentence into a learning experience." He enlisted me to help him assemble an archive of representations of mental disorder in film, art, and literature. *Crazy Talk* previewed how Gabe expected to use this "atlas of madness," as we called it. The pilot includes sampled footage from Hollywood films about mental illness such as *Vanilla Sky*, *One Flew Over the Cuckoo's Nest*, and *A Clockwork Orange*. Gabe wove these materials with news clippings about contemporary forms of madness, interviews with psychiatrists, laypeople, and the homeless, along with special effects and his mother's eeriest music to simulate deranged perceptions. The longer film would include images of madness from every culture and time, weaving the images of Goya, Blake, and Hieronymus Bosch together with Nebuchadnezzar and the crazy gods and goddesses of antiquity.

Gabe thought his film would transform the valence of madness from negative to positive and make it a critical framework for understanding all human experience, rather than a label that stigmatizes and isolates those categorized as "mentally ill." He wanted to examine the social and medical borders between sanity and madness, to see through those borders to a time when humanity could come face-to-face with its own incurable involvement in mental disorders. He liked to quote Michel Foucault's enigmatic prediction: "One day, perhaps, we will no longer know what madness was." On that day, he thought, we will see through madness, see it through to an unknown destination. His film was to provide a road map to that new world, the planet itself seen not as a violent madhouse but as a safe house, an asylum for our crazy species.

His plan was to make the film with his sister, Carmen, who was already working in film and theater in Los Angeles, struggling to find her way into the industry as a writer, actor, and director. Carmen and Gabe videotaped what was to be a planning session for the film in December of 2010. Watching this video today, I am struck by how calm and rational Gabe could be. He opens with a crisp announcement about the date with a sense that this conversation will mark the beginning of his most ambitious project. Carmen then poses the question of the film: "So, Gabriel. Why are we doing this movie?" "I guess we are just trying to get at some kind of truth," he answers. "Craziness is something that appears in every culture, in every tradition throughout history. Sometimes it is seen as evil; sometimes it's seen as good. I would like to deliver that message to an audience and be objective about it—try to show what mental illness is and is not. Just kind of lead people out of the darkness, I guess." Gabe goes on to insist on universalizing the quest for craziness as a shared human condition. And then Carmen asks him what questions about mental illness he wants to raise in the film. "I guess the question of grandiosity is interesting to me, because it has always been there. It's part of the basic process of setting goals for yourself." When Carmen presses him to clarify whether there is a difference between healthy and unhealthy forms of grandiosity, he says, "I would like to use grandiosity as a tool, because it's something I know a lot about." "Everyone has it to some degree, and what I like about it is that it is so visual, always based on some type of image . . . of what you want to be and hope to be. Of course, there is a dark side in our nightmares and worst fears," and "sometimes it is not visual, but rather a voice" that is telling us discouraging things. It can also be problematic, Gabe admits, when it involves delusional beliefs that one can do impossible things (his example is his boyhood dream of being a professional soccer player or skateboarder). But these delusions, he argues, are a human universal. Although they can be self-destructive, "they can be turned into a tool that transforms craziness into a rite of passage rather than a terminal illness," he insists. Grandiosity might be dangerous for some people with a mental illness, but not for him. As for his own condition as a certified victim of mental illness, he often declared that his mission was to be a virtuosic mental patient: "If I'm going to be crazy," he said, "I want to be really good at it. I want to be the Michael Jordan of crazy."

As the conversation continued, the focus shifted from the film project toward Gabe's own experience of mental illness and particularly his attitude toward the diagnosis of schizophrenia and the therapies associated with it. It soon becomes clear that his virtuosity as a mental patient is deeply impatient and mainly expressed as resistance to the entire framework of mental illness. He talks about his early diagnosis of "schizotypal personality disorder" and the subsequent shift to "schizophrenia," arguing that the labels are so vague as to be virtually useless. His voice rising with anger, he mimics the vacuous interviews with therapists who insist on asking formulaic questions about how he is feeling, when the most important part of his mental life is his feeling that he is being persecuted by psychiatrists. He dismisses the medications as useless, making him feel worse, and prescribed against his will. "If I refuse the medication, I lose my benefits, my housing, and my freedom." By the end of the discussion, all his skills of reasoning seem to be weaving a set of paradoxical traps. He complains that his denials that he has schizophrenia are taken as evidence that he has it—nothing but symptoms of "denial." He has PTSD, he insists, not schizophrenia. But no one believes his story about the traumatic head injury and coma he suffered twenty years ago at age sixteen. Why? Because he kept it secret all these years to protect his family from revenge by the gangbangers who injured him. Even worse, if he talks about the trauma, it forces him to remember it, and that brings it all back. He wants to forget it and get on with his life. Why should his life be defined by a single moment of trauma? Why should he have to live as a victim? At this point, his use of PTSD as an escape from the label of schizophrenia has turned into a new trap. He compares himself to a GI returning from Afghanistan, only without the benefit of having the visible scars to justify his condition. He seems to accept the labels of mental illness one minute, only to deny them the next. He is filled with rage against those who he thinks caused the illness and also against those who claim to have a cure for it. The only way out is his filmmaking, which will reveal "a truth that psychiatry and medical science has not been able to see. I want to show what madness is, from inside and outside, up, down, and sideways."

As I write, seven years after his death, Carmen is at work on a film about Gabe's life, assembling the hundreds of pages of scripts, drawings, and hours of videotape that he left behind into a biopic that will show his mission in the medium he most favored. Meanwhile, these words will have to do.

* * *

Gabe was born on July 25, 1973, in Columbus, Ohio, where I was in my first job teaching English at Ohio State University and Janice was teaching and pursuing an advanced degree in musical composition. He was born into a world of mad political turmoil, the long 1960s that persisted into the '70s. In the week he was born, John Dean was testifying about the existence of the Nixon tapes, and the yearlong countdown to the president's impeachment and resignation began. The era of Vietnam and the civil rights movement were still vividly present in the immediate past. Janice and I were radicals and hippies on alternate weekends, antiwar demonstrators and experimenters in communal living. In our student days in Baltimore during the mid-1960s, we made regular trips to protests in Washington, DC, and occasional excursions into rural Maryland for consciousness-raising. I was writing my dissertation on William Blake, and Janice was creating wild vocal settings to Wallace Stevens's "Emperor of Ice Cream": "Let be be finale of seem / The only Emperor is the Emperor of Ice Cream." We made an experimental film entitled *Metaphorsis*, a psychedelic story of a young man's journey through a world of special effects that rendered the perceptions of a "split personality," accompanied by Janice's soaring electronic soundtrack. We were basically treating life itself as a revolutionary experiment with our relationship and ourselves. When we moved to Columbus in 1968, we felt that we were living in the midst of a new American revolution, echoed by the student uprisings in Paris. Assassinations, massacres, Days of Rage, impeachment, flag-draped coffins, Kent State, drugs, sex, and rock and roll. As a duly certified scholar of British Romantic literature (with a fresh new dissertation on William Blake's art and poetry), I was sure that we were living in a period very much like Blake's, with Bob Dylan's "music in the cafés at night and revolution in the air" ringing in our ears. Wordsworth's description of the era of the French Revolution, when it was "bliss in that dawn to be alive / But to be young was very heaven," seemed equally true of our 1960s. In my classes I was teaching utopian literature and science fiction, and assuring my students that a new version of Blake's marriage of heaven and hell was right around the corner.

The October 1970 arrival of our daughter Carmen sobered us up a bit. I stopped riding a motorcycle, and Janice made me trade in my beloved 1965 Mustang convertible (on which I had squandered a year's fellowship stipend) for a safe but boring Volvo station wagon. But we also thought of Carmen as our Aquarian Age child, lulled in the womb by the sounds of the Rolling Stones and the Beatles, Aretha Franklin, Otis Redding, and the folk musicians brought to town by our dear friend Pat Mullen, founder of folklore studies at Ohio State. He once brought a wonderful but unknown slide guitar player named Sam Bowles to Columbus for a music festival and asked if Bowles could stay at our house. Of course, we agreed, and at breakfast the next morning Sam got out his dobro and regaled our one-year-old Carmen with "She's My Curly Headed Baby," while he downed a six-pack from our fridge and Carmen smeared her face with oatmeal. Carmen was to be the forerunner of a new generation, we imagined, that would be even more experimental than ourselves, would actually build the utopias we were envisioning.

I became faculty adviser to the Ohio State chapter of Students for a Democratic Society, and we founded a chapter of the New University Conference (NUC), the faculty counterpart to SDS. Our group organized an unofficial election for the new president of Ohio State (comedian Dick Gregory and scholar-activist Staughton Lynd were our candidates) that included a televised debate and mobile voting booths that ran through the halls of classroom buildings and the university hospital, where everyone from nurses to janitors to students and faculty were encouraged to vote. With Jeff Yapalater, the vice president of Ohio State's student government, we staged the "Thomas Jefferson Yapalater Starship," a roving performance group that dressed up in Founding Fathers' drag and accompanied the roving voting booths with the music of the Jefferson Airplane and a comic skit about the rebirth of democracy "right here in River City." About twenty thousand people voted. Staughton Lynd won and promptly named Dick Gregory as his vice president. The election was covered by national networks but steadfastly ignored by the OSU Board of Trustees.

By the time Gabe arrived in 1973, we were starting to think of the '60s as over. A rumor circulated at Ohio State that the era of hallucinogens and "uppers" had been replaced by a new, government-sponsored regime of "downers" and soporifics. One night at a concert I witnessed a stoned-out student staggering toward me and falling facedown onto the marble floor of the lobby with a sickening smack. He bounced back up grinning through a bloody nose and broken teeth, oblivious to what he had just done. I felt something turning.

NUC turned to more modest ambitions than a new American revolution and began organizing a Community Union to defend renters against landlords. We began research for a history of the sadly postponed American revolution at Ohio State, where the free speech movement of the early '60s had launched a generation of activism that preceded our arrival in Columbus. I started paying attention to the tenure clock and gave up my nascent career as an experimental filmmaker to turn my Blake dissertation into a book.

Who, what was Gabriel? For Carmen, he was a precious toy and playmate that we had made as a present for her. For Janice and me, he was a combination of joy and frustration, filled with humor, anger, and a dreamy moodiness. He could sit for an hour staring out our front window, sucking his thumb and curling his hair. Much later he would look back at our baby pictures of him in this position and tell us he was always seeing and hearing things that other people didn't. He was a bright but indifferent student who seemed to instinctively

FIGURE 1. Gabe at window, sucking thumb and curling hair (1975/76). Author's photograph.

resist being taught anything, while taking in everything. He could name the make, model, and year of every car on the road before he could do his times table. We once staged a contest between Carmen and Gabe to see who could be the one to make us laugh first. Carmen pulled out all her best jokes and funny faces while we sat stone-faced. Then Gabe got up and marched purposefully across the kitchen and, without breaking stride or a smile, stepped into the garbage can, a move worthy of Harpo Marx or Charlie Chaplin. We completely lost it.

Gabe became the darling of our extended family, rapidly evolving from his baby nicknames ("Booty Butt" and "Wonderbelly") into the identity that stuck right through adolescence: "Mr. Cute." He had two grandmas vying for his affection. He regarded my mother, Leona, as the cuddler who had taught him the meaning of unconditional love, while Janice's mother, Florence, was his teacher of languages and social graces. Florence graciously accepted his tutelage in the fine points of NFL football; Gabe phoned her long-distance during the Super Bowl and patiently explained terms such as downs, extra points, and sacks. Neither grandma could understand it any better than we could when he began to fall ill. "He is so bright," they would say. "Why can't he just settle down and be happy?"

Gabe was especially attached to Janice's father, Rocco. My own father, the mythic "Grandpa Tom," existed only in family legends and faded photographs as an adventurous miner and freelance prospector who had roamed the Yukon territory in the 1930s but who had died long before Gabe was born, when I was five years old. Rocco was a high school science teacher who achieved family fame by releasing thousands of fruit flies into Florence's kitchen and distilling homemade anisette in the school lab. He achieved public fame in Newark, New Jersey, by taking over as principal of the Education Center for Youth, a high school for dropouts, and turning the school into a major success for college placement in a few short years. We didn't need to harangue Carmen and Gabe about finishing their dinners. Rocco oversaw their Clean Your Plate Club, complete with framed certificates that would be awarded for the cleanest plates. He gave the kids high-quality rag paper and a starter calligraphy set so they could design their own certificates. This sort of strategy worked like a charm at his high school in Newark as well.

Gabe and Rocco first bonded over silliness and teasing, from miscounting the number of Gabe's fingers and toes (somehow there was always an extra) to water fights and pie throwing to an elusive bundle of birthday presents that was lowered and raised from the dining room chandelier just beyond Gabe's eager reach on his third birthday. The more lasting bond was Rocco's conviction that poetry and the arts and the sciences were all one quest for truth. He was Mr. Wizard at the kitchen table and a poet with epic ambitions right alongside a mastery of doggerel verse for birthdays and anniversaries, and elegies for the passing generations of our dogs: "How soon our Sheba's race was run."

In the summer of 1977, when we had just moved to Chicago, Rocco and Florence came to help us move in, and he and four-year-old Gabe set about washing our kitchen windows from the outside. I decided to film them at work with my ever-ready movie camera, and Rocco began pretending to wash the space left by an open window, as if there were an invisible pane of glass that needed polishing. Gabe immediately began thrusting his arm through the nonexistent glass, and Rocco, pretending to admonish him, pulled Gabe's arm back and shook a reproving finger at him every time he penetrated the imaginary pane.

No doubt this scene stands out in my memory because I captured it in a precious home movie. But it also haunts me in the way it played with illusion and reality, with Rocco encouraging a four-year-old to act the role of reality check to his crazy, loveable grandpa.

My own relation to Gabe was filled with grandiose hopes and frequent frustration. When he was born, the idea of having a son filled me with visions of possible futures—perhaps he would be a great athlete eager to be molded by me. As a modestly talented but nearsighted wide receiver who had declined a football scholarship at Central Michigan University in favor of an academic scholarship at Michigan State, I was resigned to being a spectator who "could have been a contender." But Gabe was going to have the advantage, I thought, of systematic fatherly coaching from a very early age. I planned regular drills in eye-hand coordination, agility training, strength coaching, and careful attention to the most arcane rules of baseball—force outs, infield fly rules, when not to bunt. I was quickly disabused of this ambition, and his resistance to being taught anything by anyone probably started with my clumsy coaching. In our games of catch, the ball would inevitably pop out of his glove and hit him on the nose, ending the practice session right there.

I found out how delicate and difficult it can be for a father to teach his son, especially for someone like me, whose father died when he was five years old, leaving me with nothing but a tin of his ashes that I buried in our backyard and my mother's oft-repeated legends about being swept away by him on their first date. He was an outsize figure in my memories of childhood, the heroic mining engineer with a bush pilot's license who flew with me in a Piper Cub over Los Angeles when I was four years old. He was a man of the world who knew all about rocks and railroads and had lifted me up into the cab of a roaring steam locomotive idling at a crossing in Reno, where I was compelled to share a lunch of relish and Wonder Bread sandwiches with an engineer whose hands and face were covered in soot and grease. "Do I really have to eat this?" I whispered to my dad. "Mm-hmm," he nodded, telling me that it would be impolite to refuse.

I suppose that I wanted Gabe to see me as a legendary figure like my father, only I was determined not to abandon him by dying when he was five years old but to be there to lead him to the greater heights my own father only seemed to have promised. When I tried to engage Gabe in my own child-hood obsession with sandcastling, a surefire attraction to the crowds of kids that gathered on the beach to watch us at work, he would sometimes tune out. My focus was on the intrica-cies of the castle itself, which I treated as a temple of fragile beauty and certainly not the appropriate target of the destruc-tive impulses of a four-year-old. "Can I knock it down?" was his inevitable request when the work was done. "No, let's leave that for Lake Michigan." Or the Atlantic or the Pacific, wher-ever we happened to be. "Ah, Dad, come on." I was firm with him, perhaps remembering the lesson of the relish sandwich.

CHAPTER TWO

A *MAD* Tour

In the summer of Gabe's tenth year, we took our annual vacation in New Jersey, where we always stayed with Grandpa Rocco and Grammy Florence. The routine was well established: a day or two at the Jersey Shore bodysurfing and building sandcastles, walking the boardwalk, bingeing on calamari and pizza, cotton candy and the "all you can eat" fish special at one of the local seafood joints. Grandpa Rocco would counsel Carmen and Gabe about the economics of the buffet: "Don't bother with the bread. Fill up on the shrimp and steamers and chocolate mousse. They won't make a dime on this family!"

But this year was different. Rocco had passed away that spring after a short illness, and the world suddenly seemed very empty for all of us. Carmen was busy with Florence and Janice, so I proposed an all-boys excursion to New York with

Gabe. "What shall we do?" I asked him, using the ritual mal-apropisms we had learned from Rocco: "Shall we go to the Umpire State Building (where the most despised figures of baseball are commemorated)? The Statute of Liberty (where some law books might be stored)? Or just hang out at the Port of Authority (a place that the Misurell family always insisted on misnaming)?" "No," he said. "I want to visit *MAD* magazine." Gabe was a new subscriber and was deeply absorbed in *MAD*, right alongside a growing collection of superhero comics from Marvel and DC—Batman, Spider-Man, Superman, Captain America, the Fantastic Four, the X-Men, and G.I. Joe. I smuggled my own favorite, Wonder Woman, into his collection as well. So I telephoned the offices of *MAD* (located at a conspicuously emphasized address on "MADison Avenue"). The receptionist told me that they didn't really have a "tour" of any kind, but we were certainly welcome to drop by.

We arrived at *MAD*'s offices that afternoon—stepping off the elevator into a shabby linoleum-floored, fluorescent-lit, ten-by-ten space, with a Swedish modern sofa and chairs upholstered in cracked plastic and a coffee table strewn with old copies of *MAD* in languages (Finnish, Japanese, Turkish) that I scarcely recognized. In the corner stood a statue of Alfred E. Neuman, *MAD*'s moronic "What, me worry?" icon of clueless nerdiness with a plastic pigeon perched on his head. The receptionist, a large woman with Coke-bottle glasses, seemed too deeply absorbed in her work to bother with us. After a few minutes I got her attention and reminded her that I had called earlier in the day about a tour. She gave me a blank look, finally turning around to yell to someone in the inner offices: "Hey, that kid is here for the tour." Two men emerged from the inner sanctum, each grabbing one of Gabe's arms and lifting him from the floor. They ran him through the inner offices with his legs dangling for about a half minute, then circled back to the lobby, where they deposited him on the floor. "OK, kid. That's your tour."

It took us a heartbeat to realize that the whole thing was a put-on. They burst out laughing and said, "OK, kid. What would you really like to see?" Of course, Gabe wanted to meet artist Don Martin, editor Harvey Kurtzman, and publisher William Gaines, and all the demented artists who made *MAD* such an irresistible read for adolescent boys and their recovering adolescent fathers. But the artists, we were told, rarely showed up at the magazine's offices. "Most of them live in a nuthouse and can't be allowed to roam around free." "Really?" Gabe asked. No, not really, they admitted. They amended the story then to say that the artists worked from home in appropriate squalor and destitution and only came in to hand in their artwork because they couldn't afford postage. "So if we can't see the artists, can we see some of the original artwork?" We were led to a long row of filing cabinets adorned with labels like "Dirty Picture File"; "Obscene Picture File"; "Wacky Picture File"; and "Stupid Picture File." "How do you ever find anything?" Gabe asked. "Who said we find anything?" said our guide. "We live for the present, in a constant state of demented amnesia." Nevertheless, there was a secret order of some kind. They managed to go right to the things we wanted to see, such as the original drawings for early covers like the parody of the radio program *The Shadow* ("Who knows what evil lurks in the hearts of men?"), featuring its antihero, Shadowski-Boom-Boom. We reveled in the sketches for "Spy versus Spy" and the *MAD* parodies of *Aliens* and Tom Cruise's *Top Gun* in what was then the current issue. The editors showed us the process by which original drawings were turned into finished comics with hand-lettering and coloring.

The editors asked Gabe how old he was, and when he told them he was just ten, they nodded approvingly. "You are our target audience," they said. "Thirteen-year-old boys are the primary readership of *MAD*. If we hook you at ten, we have you for life." (As a charter subscriber, I can personally testify to the truth of this, although most sensible readers grow out of their addiction to *MAD* by age eighteen). Then they asked Gabe how he liked the tour. He answered, "It was cool—really a great relief. I was worried that you might be all slick and corporate, but you guys are even crazier than I hoped." They complimented him on his taste and discernment, telling him that the fact that he was already a subscriber at ten could only mean one of two things: either you are really, really precocious, or you are completely out of your mind.

I think of the visit to *MAD* as one of the things that later provided Gabe with a kind of anchor memory as he struggled with the label of schizophrenia. During the onset of his illness he began to make visionary calligraphy, cartoon sequences, and enigmatic images. One of the strangest is a simple drawing of a door in which the words "Love" (green), "Identity" (purple), and "Harm" (red) are inscribed. Love, for Gabe, was the door to something beyond Identity; as for Identity, he seemed to frame it as a barrier against the danger outside, perhaps against the threat he felt of losing himself in the vortex of schizophrenia. One of his accusations against Janice and me was that we had given him too much freedom and insufficient discipline, thus failing to give him a firm identity. He thought of love as something that lay behind a closed door, a door that we could and should have opened for him. As he

FIGURE 2. Gabriel Mitchell, "Gabriel's Door: Love, Identity, Harm" (1994). Colored ink drawing.

was falling ill around age nineteen, he began kicking down doors in our house.

In May 2012, just a few weeks before Gabe's death, he immersed himself one last time in the world of comic books. My friend Hillary Chute organized a conference of avant-garde comic artists, including Art Spiegelman, R. Crumb, Alison Bechdel, and Joe Sacco. Hillary and another friend, Patrick Jagoda, had come together at Gabe's prompting as the core members of a tiny "Superhero Film Society" focused on the convergence of DC and Marvel with cinematic spectacle. Our preference was for "flawed" superheroes, such as Batman (depression), Wolverine (misanthropy), Dark Phoenix (psychosis), and Spider-Man (anxious graduate student). Gabe was our principal guide to the superhero comics, while Hillary led us into the parallel histories of nonfiction, feminist, and autobiographical graphic narrative. She had made it her business to seek out and cultivate the leading practitioners of what we used to call "underground" comics. Patrick was our expert on videogames, and I was along for the ride, seeing it as the perfect way to have companions for all the movies that Janice could never be persuaded to see.

For Gabe, it was a chance to mingle with the gods of his idolatry, revealed as perfectly ordinary human beings. He was particularly enamored with Spiegelman, who shared a smoke with Gabe and informed him that he insisted on smoking while lecturing, partly to defy the rules but mainly "as a prop, to bring a reminder of death into the room." Spiegelman confided with him about his steadfast adherence to the wackiness and emotional immaturity of the MAD ethos. Gabe had already been creating hand-drawn autobiographical sketches of his journeys through the worlds of mental illness and addiction for his music video, *Desolation Row Revisited*, and the encounters with Phoebe Gloeckner and Alison Bechdel, comic artists who made their own experiences material for autobiographical comic books, were inspiring for him. The idea that the role of comic book hero might not be confined to musclemen and spandex-clad mutants, but could extend

FIGURE 3. Gabriel Mitchell, "Nate McClennen" (2012). Detail of a thank-you note cartoon. Ink drawing.

to skateboarders, outcasts, antiheroes, and mental patients, was deeply reassuring. Shortly after Gabe's death, his friend, cartoonist Nate McClennen, who stayed with him during the conference, wrote a graphic thank-you note that called out to the ghostly image of his fallen comrade.

What is the "proper distance" between a father and his son? Sometimes I felt rather awkwardly that I was more like an older brother to him, confusing mentoring and discipline with competition. Still, I didn't feel like an utter failure as a father, and Gabe's life prior to the onset of his illness in the early 1990s seemed within the range of a normal rebellious youth with a sweet, loving personality and outsize ambitions. A brief flirtation with therapy at the age of thirteen resulted in a diagnosis of minor depression. This seemed to pass when he left the competitive environment of the University of Chicago's Laboratory School with its Ivy League–bound students and transferred to Kenwood High School, a public school just down the street from our house, where he was a white boy doing a reasonable job of getting along in a mainly black school. He captained the soccer team, discovered a passion for psychology, and developed a reputation as a visionary spirit among his friends. He fell in love with a girl who lived a few houses away and then was banned from seeing her after he kept her out all night talking (he assured us it was just talking) about the meaning of life on the shores of Lake Michigan. When he graduated from high school in the spring of 1991, he seemed ready for college. His arrival at NYU that fall was filled with joy and anticipation. After we had unloaded his stereo system and had met his roommates and the girls in the adjacent room, he was eager for us to leave. Janice and I spent a moody half hour driving north to the George Washington Bridge and then burst into song and laughter as we crossed the bridge, realizing that we were empty nesters for the first time in twenty-one years. The "homeless" phone call a few months later was a bit concerning, but only after the onset of his illness became official did its significance dawn on us. Many years later, in the days immediately after Gabe's death, it was one of the first things I recollected.

In the next three years, after that homeless phone call, from 1991 to 1994, Gabe went through increasingly extreme cycles of enthusiasm and despair. He fell in love with a girl named Cricket, who became an obsession for him that led to his being accused of stalking. He became a philosopher, discovered the meaning of life, concluded that it was meaningless without Cricket, got kicked out of school, returned briefly on probation, withdrew indefinitely, and became a different person. His sister, Carmen, returning from her junior year abroad in London, described the difference: "My funny, sweet, warm-hearted brother was replaced by this hostile, suspicious, humorless being, full of paranoia and accusation, staring straight ahead, unblinking." Gabe's self-characterization on his website, Philmworx.com, is a bit more lighthearted: "Hopefully you have a strong stomach, now watch as the artist does a strip tease with his own life story. Look no further true believers—it is here that you can witness the first coming of the second banana." He also enumerated his own superpowers, namely, the ability to "smoke cigarettes and drink coffee at the same time" and "the mutant ability to get kicked out of prestigious universities."

Aside from the mildly alarming phone call about becoming homeless, Gabe seemed to do well in his first year at NYU. He was becoming infatuated with philosophy, quoting St. Augustine and Plato to us. We figured that, like almost every freshman, he would be smoking pot (we later learned there was a lot more, with bowls of pills available at parties). He also seemed to be making friends, and his one-sided romance with Cricket did not seem to be a problem. When he came home for the summer of 1992, he took a job at the Seminary Co-op Bookstore and coached kids in soccer summer camp. But a warning signal flashed in late July when we left him at home for two weeks while we took a trip to Europe. He took LSD with some friends and decided to show them that he could fly. He jumped off the back deck of our house, a ten-foot drop, and seriously injured his foot. We hoped this would be a lesson, about both drugs and flying. A passionate skateboarder, he was a compulsive risk-taker who didn't seem to mind leaving his skin on the "beautiful hips"—his

AND NOT JUST THE OPINION OF THOSE ON DESOLATION ROW

FIGURE 4. Gabriel Mitchell, "Angelic skateboarder showering money on homeless" (n.d.). From *Desolation Row Revisited*.

name for the high curbs in Chicago's downtown underpasses. "Road rash" was his scabby badge of honor. Later he made films about the hips, accompanied by voice over exclamations about his need to "fly, fly, fly."

In the fall of 1992, things began to fall apart at NYU. His childhood friend Alex came to stay with him, and Gabe supplied him with some marijuana that produced a bad reaction. This came to the attention of the dorm authorities, and he was put on probation. Then it turned out he was skipping classes and homework and trying to bring the homeless into the dorm. By the end of November, it was clear that he needed to take a leave, and we brought him home for the winter and spring of 1993. I had accepted a three-month research residency at Caltech for the winter, and Janice joined me there, so once again he was living at home alone. He began phoning Cricket's mother, who lived in Chicago, on the theory that the way to Cricket's heart must be through her mother. But he returned to the bookstore job, and we were finally able, from a distance, to convince him to see a psychiatrist.

CHAPTER THREE

The Therapeutic Landscape

Gabe was deeply resistant to seeing a doctor of any kind. He would stonewall therapists or go on a tirade about the "real problem" (friends and family who would not help him reunite with Cricket). But after a close personal friend who had known him since childhood recommended Dr. L, a highly qualified psychiatrist, Gabe agreed to see him twice a week while we were in California. When we returned in March, Dr. L suggested that I come in for a consultation. After an hour with Gabe, Dr. L invited me into his office. "Gabe, please tell your father what you have been telling me."

"I don't know why you brought me here, Dad. There is nothing wrong with me. I am just trying to escape the straitjacket you and Mom have put me in. And now you bring me to this so-called doctor, and he is probably tape-recording this conversation now to use it against me." Gabe's flagrant display of paranoia overwhelmed me. I couldn't speak. The energy seemed to rush out of my body, and I started sobbing. Dr. L handed me a box of tissues, and I found myself wondering how many boxes he used in a week of sessions. So many tears in a place like this. Why had we come? Was this really happening? "Gabe," said Dr. L, "Don't you see how upset your father is? Do you really think he wants to confine you? Do you really believe that there is a hidden tape recorder somewhere in my office?" "It's probably right there," said Gabe, pointing at the light fixture on the ceiling. "This whole thing is just a setup to take away my freedom."

Dr. L asked Gabe to wait outside for a few minutes while he talked to me. "I'll put it to you straight," he said. "Your son has a thought disorder. He is paranoid and has what we call 'ideas of reference,' which means that he thinks everything in the world is a signal directed at him. He is filled with anger and has a real potential for hurting himself or others. My prediction is that he will either wind up in jail or in a hospital. He will need long-term therapy and will have to be medicated." "So what do we do?" I asked. "Make sure he winds up in a hospital, not jail. You need to construct a safety net to be ready for the break that is surely going to come."

But it didn't, not right away. Gabe settled into a routine at the bookstore and started art therapy, which did little for his moods but produced a whole series of striking drawings and calligraphic improvisations, as if he were trying to invent a new writing system. Most of his anger was directed at Janice, mainly expressed in slamming and kicking doors and then breaking down crying. Occasionally, however, he would switch to a manic or (more precisely) a comic mood, coming into the kitchen with a wastebasket on his head, or clowning around with Lucy and C.C., enjoying the unconditional love of our two obstreperous mutts. And when we had a weeklong visit with friends from France, he suddenly seemed to snap out of all the unhappiness and anger and act like the wonderfully smart and sweet young man that we had known until he went to college. But later in the summer, when he joined us on a long drive to Boston, something snapped, and he refused to come out of the car on a one-hundred-degree day at the beach, smoldering with anger at Janice and me.

The big breakdown that Dr. L predicted didn't materialize. In the spring of 1993, I took Gabe with me on a trip to France. I had become convinced that the best medicine for him would be close father-son times. I believed I could pull him out of his depression by taking him camping, going to movies, and watching and playing sports together.

We flew to Paris in early June, where we had a layover for one night. We walked in the Luxembourg Gardens and the effect on him was magical as we read the famous names on the monuments to Delacroix and Marie di Medici. "Dad, you have to promise me that the next time we come to Paris we will go to the grave of Jim Morrison and leave a poem or a bottle of whiskey." The music of the Doors was part of our common DNA, haunted especially by the lyrics of "When the Music's Over" and Morrison's primal scream: "Father, I want to kill you. Mother, I want to aaauuugggghhhh. . . ." We seemed to be having a mystical experience of some kind, or perhaps it was just our shared jet lag.

We then met philosopher Jacques Derrida and his wife, Marguerite, for dinner near our hotel and shared a quiet evening. Gabe asked Jacques to explain his famous concept of "deconstruction." "Is it true," he asked, "that you think words have no meaning?" "No, that is not what I think," replied Jacques. "That is something they say in the newspapers.

I think it is exactly the opposite; words have too much meaning, and deconstruction exposes their layers." Gabe was completely thrilled by this answer. "Are words like birds, then? Or more like turds?" Jacques smiled. "Perhaps both?" Gabe then told him, "When I was a kid, I used to annoy my parents by asking 'why' all the time. And then when they told me to stop, I liked to ask, 'Why do I ask why all the time?'" Jacques laughed and said, "That is exactly what philosophers do."

Gabe loved wordplay and had learned the art of nonsense from the master, his grandpa Rocco. Every escalator at a department store was immediately turned into an alligator, a perilous ridge-backed reptile, with Jim Morrison's "Ride the snake" echoing in mind. The name of every city was mutilated: "Newark" became "Nurk," and "Columbus" became "Clumps." We sang the names of the states, asking, "What did Della Wear?" and answering that, of course, she wore her "New Jersey." When Santa came to "Clumps, Ahia," on Christmas he shouted "Ho Hi Ho" as he came down our chimney. The recitation of ABC's was regularly disrupted: "ABCDEF—POOPIE!" His favorite names for me were "Dadzilla" and "Dadriel." Janice was "Mamacita" and "Momice." Carmen was "Carsister" and "Carwomyn." His friend Alex was "Dr. Strangefreund."

Gabe was comfortable with Derrida because he had met the great philosopher at our home the previous spring and had introduced him to Monty Python's comedy sketch, "The Philosophers' Football Match," between the Ancients (Socrates, Aristotle, Plotinus, etc.) and the Moderns (Descartes, Kant, Hegel, Marx, and Nietzsche). After Jacques recovered from a fit of laughter over Marx's red card, and Nietzsche's expulsion from the game, Gabe asked the critical question: "Whose side are you on?" "The Ancients, of course," Jacques replied. "Does that mean that deconstruction is on the side of ancient philosophy?" "Yes," Jacques said. "Deconstruction is not something you decide to do; it is something that happens, whether you like it or not." "Is it like death, then?" said Gabe. "Perhaps," said Jacques. "Or like debt, for sure. Maybe like justice, if we are lucky."

As our Paris dinner proceeded, Marguerite Derrida began to draw Gabe out, and Gabe described his dreams and ambitions as an artist and filmmaker. Marguerite, a practicing psychotherapist, nodded sympathetically as Gabe spoke of his plans to take a meeting with Spike Lee and his ambition to walk the red carpet at the Academy Awards. He explained that he was making all our home movies in CinemaScope so that they would be ready for the Oscar competition. As we walked back to our hotel, Marguerite took my arm. "Tell me about your son." "The jet lag was probably getting to him," I said, cautiously but truthfully. "He has great ambitions and sometimes gets ahead of himself." Gabe walked ahead, arm-in-arm with Derrida in animated conversation.

The next morning we flew to Nice, where I was speaking at a conference. We were met at the airport and taken to the local university for a reception. As I mingled with the crowd, I noticed that Gabe was missing and went searching for him. I found him huddled under a staircase sobbing. I tried to get him to talk, but he flared with anger. When I tried to hold him, he pushed me away. "*You* of all people should know what's wrong!" he said. I was supposed to understand perfectly what was upsetting him, and I knew that whatever it was, it was my fault.

When he finally calmed down, I went to the organizer of the conference and told him that my son was not feeling well, and we needed to check into our hotel immediately. But when the driver arrived at the hotel, it turned out to be a shabby place, a thirty-minute taxi drive across the city from the conference location. At this point, I was ready to take the first flight back to Chicago. We returned to the reception, where I explained that we would have to stay where the conference was taking place because I could not leave my son alone all day. They readily agreed, and Gabe and I were driven to the conference venue, a nineteenth-century monastery on Pointe de Gaton, perched on a cliff overlooking the Mediterranean Sea. We were shown into a bare, high-ceilinged guest room filled with darkness, slivers of sunlight beaming through shutters at the far end. Gabe went to the window and threw open the shutters with a gasp. We could see fifty miles out to sea and look down at the waves crashing on the rocks at the foot of the cliff. I photographed Gabe just as he took his shirt off and stood gazing out the window. "Oh, Dad," he said. "I feel so much better."

The rest of the sojourn was mostly giddy happiness. We gathered up our snorkeling equipment, climbed down a stairway carved in the cliff, and plunged into the warm clear water. We basked in the sun smiling at each other furtively as we pretended not to notice the gorgeous young French women showering topless a few yards from us. We agreed that this is what sunglasses were really invented for.

The conference then dissolved into a haze of delicious seafood, wine, and sunshine. On the last day we rented a car and drove the upper corniche, singing the theme songs to James Bond movies, swerving around hairpin curves a thousand feet above the sea, imagining ourselves in hot pursuit of one of Bond's criminal masterminds. Along for the ride was one of my American colleagues from the conference, a woman in her thirties. Gabe drew her out about her work and personal life and told her of his dream of being a great film director,

FIGURE 5. Gabe at window, Pointe de Gaton, Nice (June 1993). Author's photograph.

all of which she enthusiastically supported. He instantly fell in love with her and as we stopped to gaze out at the view, he asked her to marry him. She told him how attractive he was, that he was sure to make some lucky woman very happy, but that she already had an attachment. Later that evening, Gabe complained that she hadn't taken him seriously.

After our trip to France, I began to think that the best medicine for Gabe might be as simple as scenery—beautiful, interesting places. Perhaps he just needed therapeutic landscapes. I recalled the trip we made to New Mexico when he was nine years old. We camped in national parks (Mesa Verde, Bandelier, Canyon de Chelly) and immersed ourselves in the lore of the vanished Anasazi Indians. At the end of the trip, Gabe and Carmen informed us that they did not want to go home but wanted to continue living among the relics of the cliff dwellers. Could a change of scenery and a removal from our increasingly toxic home environment be the answer? In the midst of the horrors of summer 1994 (Janice was diagnosed with breast cancer and my sister died from brain cancer), on the glide path toward the psychotic break we could feel coming, we sent him off to stay in New Jersey with his teenage cousins, Justin, Michael, and Travis. He had known these boys since they were babies and could play the role of older brother with them, cruising the Jersey Shore, fishing for crabs in Barnegat Bay, and doing somersaults on the backyard trampoline. With light supervision by his doting Aunt Patti and Uncle Mizzie, he spent a month there—probably the last episode of happiness before the hospitalization that was coming at the end of summer. His young adolescent cousins adored him and looked up to him as almost-but-not-too-much a grownup, a twenty-one-year-old who was happy to hang around with them. Years later, remembering these times with Gabe, his cousins recalled it as one of their best summers ever. Cousin Gabe was "a bit unusual" but all the more delightful for that.

Gabe was great with children because he could be on their level—silly, playful, rambunctious. But this would also create problems when he could not establish a proper distance from them. At one family gathering when he was roughhousing with his young cousins, they all began climbing on him, and the laughter suddenly turned to tears when he got very upset with them, acting as if he couldn't defend himself. Then he became angry with me because I wouldn't defend him. I told him that it was important for him to defend himself and to assert his adult privileges when play became too rough. "You're my father," he said. "I expect you to defend me."

We began to think that it was our family situation that was toxic to him. Carmen had moved to Seattle, and he had become an only child with a very uncertain future. So we decided it was time to see a family therapist together to work on the dynamic of our daily relations with him. We engaged Dr. B, who provided a somewhat comforting narrative based in his experience working in our racially mixed neighborhood of Hyde Park, where liberal, bourgeois academic and professional families are the norm. Your son is just an immature twenty-year-old with a mild case of depression, we were told. He is just testing his parents. Dr. B said we needed to give Gabe some tough love and set boundaries. "It's nothing but man-ip-u-la-tion," he said, stressing each syllable. This stiffened our resolve to stop taking shit from him. So we made a contract that stipulated if Gabe held a job, finished his incompletes, and stopped drinking and smoking weed, we would let him go back to NYU. Surprisingly, he kept his side of the agreement to the letter, and we began making plans for his return in the winter of 1994.

It was a measure of how eager we were to get him out of the house and let him go back to school that we minimized some disturbing behaviors. He began to remodel our house, beginning with his own room, where he removed the faces of his drawers and then reattached them with hinges. He gathered up a dozen old wooden shutters in the basement and began encasing our furnace with them. Door slamming and kicking increased, and it seemed to us that he was quite literally trying to break through walls and break out of our house. Given the prospect of returning to school, this seemed to make sense, and we hoped the return would provide a real version of that breakout.

We also tried a bit of proactive family therapy in the form of tape-recording our conversations. The idea was to play back to him the things he was saying when he was agitated, so that he could reflect on them when he had calmed down. His paranoia about his friends and family was getting increasingly intense, and we worried that he was going to have no friends if he didn't learn to control his temper. We told him that we were recording these conversations, and at first he seemed confident that they would show how unreasonable we were being. But he also quickly accused us of doing it in order to use them against him.

A few days after Christmas, Gabe experienced a kind of hysterical episode in which he lay in bed shivering and moaning, paralyzed, unable to walk, and complaining that he was going blind. When Janice tried to take his temperature, he became agitated and told her to leave him alone. We finally had to call an ambulance, and he was taken to the emergency room, where (after a quick recovery from the paralysis) they said he might have been suffering from severe flu symptoms. We of course began to doubt the advisability of his returning to NYU. So a few days later we decided to tape a conversation on precisely this subject. One evening after dinner I switched on the tape recorder and asked him if he had called a particular administrator to discuss the paperwork necessary for his return. Already annoyed that the recorder was running, he exploded with anger. "I tried to call him three times and couldn't get through. Why are you bugging me about this? Do you want me to go stick my head up his butt and see if he has a disease?" I tried to remain calm: "Don't you think it's time to start thinking seriously about your return to NYU?" "I have been thinking about it." His voice was filled with fury, turning sentences into long crescendos, higher and louder. "Thinking about something and doing it in this house are problems." He then changed the subject to his hospitalization: "Since you dragged me to the hospital for no reason whatsoever," we had, he said, humiliated him "unceremoniously" (Gabe was never at a loss for words). "By force of law, I was put in an ambulance." "You still don't have any remorse for what you've done." He dismissed Janice's attempt to take his temperature during the paralysis episode as an assault on his autonomy: "A sentient personality can do it for themselves."

He then went to a theme that was to recur often: "Why did you bring me into the world if you just wanted to make me unhappy? You don't go making a sandcastle and then knock it down. Then why would you make a son and then make him miserable?" Janice reminded him that we were planning to let him go back to school, which should be making him happy. After all, he had fulfilled his side of the contract, to which he replied, "This contract is food for the fireplace as far as I am concerned. School is not the answer, it is meaningless; there is no future in it." When I said, "But I thought you wanted to go back," he answered, "I want to go back. I've always wanted to go back, but what I want and what is actually going to happen are two different things. I wish you would go away. How about that?" When Janice said, "You could leave us, you know—no one is stopping you," his response was a long silence. I finally broke it by telling him that it was no longer clear to me that he wanted to go back to school. His answer: "Well, I'm not clear about something, too. How you can be so unclear?" My response: "When I listen to you, I am not sure what I am hearing." His: "You seem to have instant perspective on everything I espouse. You have been sticking your hand in front of my eyes every time I try to go." He then accused Janice of constantly hurting his feelings, and when she pointed out how nasty and hurtful he was being, he shouted at her, "You have no feelings! Why did you bring me into the world if you are going to treat me this way? You don't know the meaning of the word 'nasty.' You are degrading yourself by naming yourself as a mother. If you wanted another child, that should mean by definition that you fulfill the requisite of that want."

Then he gave us the clearest account so far of what he meant by "the requisite of that want." It turned out to be his obsessive, one-sided love for Cricket, which now burst into full bloom. Gabe was convinced that Cricket was being held hostage by her mother—"she wants her to be a nun"—or by "complete strangers" who had rudely intervened when he tried to express his love for her, or by a "supposed lawyer"—perhaps not a fantasy—who had laid hands on Gabe and threatened him with a lawsuit for stalking. The worst persecutors were Janice and me, preventing him from seeing Cricket or failing to work as a go-between to repair their damaged love affair.

I had to wait for several years after his death before I could bear to listen to these tapes, the delusions and obsessions pouring out with all the rhetoric of blame and guilt. As guilty liberals, a Russian Jew and an Irish Catholic, Janice and I were very good at blaming ourselves, accusing ourselves of not doing enough. Gabe really understood our vulnerabilities: "You are . . . the people preventing me from getting to her. Someone has poisoned her mind against me, telling her that I am a rapist and a stalker. Why should I be kept apart from the person I love?"

All the romantic idealism in Gabe's young psyche had been poured into his obsession with this young woman, who, so far as we could tell, had little inkling of how her image had taken over his life. He portrayed their relationship in visionary watercolors as a mythic romance, as if they were the last couple on earth, or a new Adam and Eve who would procreate an emancipated human race after the millennial deluge. He

FIGURE 6. Gabriel Mitchell, "Gabe and Cricket standing on wave" (ca. 1998). Watercolor.

depicted them as a couple standing calmly at the crest of an enormous purple wave that seems to be breaking *away* from the shore into an abyss of blue. The drawing perfectly captures the precarious combination of calm certainty and imminent disaster that characterized his feelings about Cricket.

Gabe's most detailed reflection on his idealization of Cricket appeared at about the same time (1998), in his film script *American Dreamers*. In a dialogue with Janice and me, he writes these lines for himself, explaining how Cricket fits into his life plan.

> I feel like I could do anything. If I was to become a homeless person, I would be the greatest homeless person the world had ever seen. If I was religious I would become a saint. If I went into business I would be the richest man who ever lived. I could do anything I set my mind to, I have some kind of power that I can't fully comprehend. I have so much good energy right now, I feel like I could go for a walk and never stop for anything. I feel like the whole universe is my oyster, and in that universe, even with all that cosmic power, I just want to be with Cricket. She's beautiful and mysterious. I want to discover her intricacies, explain her complexities, I feel like she's the answer to every question I've ever asked. And if I find out her meaning, I find out the meaning of life.

We learned to dread the sound of Cricket's name as the sure sign of a relapse into delusions. No amount of wise fatherly advice about how I had dealt with a broken heart in my day could shake Gabe's conviction that Cricket was secretly yearning for him—or worse, conspiring to tease him with encouraging signals in order to destroy his life. Cricket was both his angelic ideal and femme fatale, an ambivalent complex that became a central theme of Gabe's later screenplays, where she was replaced by the figure of Cameron Diaz, especially her portrayal of Tom Cruise's diabolical "fuck buddy" in one of Gabe's favorite films, *Vanilla Sky*. The only alternative to his shattered love that Gabe ever accepted as an explanation for his unhappiness was a narrative of physical trauma, a shattered *skull* and concussion administered by his own comrades during a gang confrontation. But that was a different, later story.

Talking with your paranoid offspring is hard work. We learned to anticipate huge leaps of logic (you gave me life and are therefore responsible for my happiness), appeals to justice (no one has the right to deprive me of the woman I love), and trigger words (love, reality, grandiosity . . . just about anything could light a fuse). At moments of absurdity, the conversation sometimes exploded in bursts of laughter. Once when Janice had spent an hour fielding one of his harangues, she had had enough, and as she tried to withdraw from the conversation he began to be even more abusive, accusing her of refusing even to communicate with him. I broke in by saying, "Shall I take over the next shift?" Gabe laughed, but as the joke sank in, he turned sour: "So I'm a job, am I? You made me, and now you are stuck with the mess you made."

The general tenor of these non-conversations, then, was hurtful verbal violence, punctuated by luminous moments of shared absurdity. We were uncaring and deceptive failures in his eyes, yet at the same time idealized as the only people capable of saving him. That was the measure of our failure. It was a grueling experience that I have mostly tried to forget in these pages. I am amazed in listening to the tapes again how calm Janice and I were. We tried to listen to him carefully, to respond as directly and truthfully as possible, to ignore the insults and obscenities, while trying to bring him into the present moment as much as possible—and guide him toward therapy.

CHAPTER FOUR

"There's Something in My Head"

A deal is a deal. Despite all these warning signs, we let Gabe return to NYU in the winter of 1994. We were comforted by the fact that he would not be staying in the NYU dormitories but in Brooklyn with our oldest and dearest friend, Florence Tager, who had known Gabe since he was a baby. Like a sister to Janice and to me, and "Auntie Flo" to our children, Florence had been one of our co-conspirators in the New University Conference when we were making revolution at Ohio State before she left to teach education at Medgar Evers College in Brooklyn. Gabe's childhood was filled with memories of Florence joining us on holidays. She was "extended family," the sort of situation that had always suited him best. His relation to his nuclear family was just that: nuclear. This arrangement, we told ourselves, would give him a secure refuge away from the frenetic atmosphere of the NYU campus. It would effectively keep him from hanging out with homeless people in Washington Square, taking drugs, and hassling Cricket. All these comforting thoughts turned out to be mistaken. Gabe's condition quickly deteriorated. He was accused of stalking Cricket, and he started acting weirdly around Florence, sleeping with a baseball bat next to his bed and eavesdropping obtrusively on the meetings of her women's reading group. After some weeks, she called me to say that she didn't feel safe around him. Florence was in mourning for her recently deceased mother and was in no condition to deal with a young man who was becoming impossible for us to live with. I think we hoped that Gabe's ability to conceal his symptoms outside the nuclear family would work with Florence, but to him, she too had become radioactive.

I called to tell him that he could no longer stay with Florence, but he refused to consider moving to alternative housing, an option that seemed problematic to us in any case. I told him he was going to have to withdraw from school again and come home. When he adamantly refused, I had no other options. I got on the first available plane and flew to New York to fetch him. I stepped into a bubble of numbness, going through all the travel motions like a robot. When I arrived at Florence's apartment, he was surprised to see me.

"What are you doing here?"

"I've come to take you back to Chicago," I said.

"Not happening, dude. This is where I live, and you can't make me leave."

"Gabe," I said, "this is Florence's apartment, and she doesn't want you living with her anymore."

"Let her move out, then," he said. "I'm doing fine. She's the one whose life is all fucked up with her radical women's groups. All they do is yak about how terrible men are."

I threatened to call the police if he wouldn't come with me voluntarily. He took that as a cue to run out of the apartment into the blizzard of 1994, one of the worst in New York history. The drifts were up to the parking meters, and the sidewalks were narrow trenches.

I chased him through the streets of Park Slope, determined not to let him out of my sight. Somewhere around Grand Army Plaza he realized I was still behind him, and he turned to face me, all furious defiance. I stood face-to-face with him and tried to find my son behind his blank, staring eyes. He reached down and picked up a large block of ice and held it over his head. For reasons I will never know, I was not afraid that he would throw it at me. I called his bluff. "I don't think you want to hurt me," I said. It was a lucky hunch. He hesitated, exhaled, a flash of light coming from his eyes, and dropped the ice.

We walked in silence back to Florence's apartment. When I tried to put my arm around him, he pushed me away. As we reached the apartment and I prepared to call a cab to take us to the airport, he announced once again that he would not leave. He dared me to make him. "What are you going to do? Drag me to the cab?" I called the police and explained the situation to them, asking them to send a psychiatric unit. In the long ten minutes between the call and their arrival, the air was filled with electricity. It felt to me as if it was sparkling and pulsating. Everything about the room was suddenly brightly lit, as if we were in a stage play, dislocated into a climactic scene out of Eugene O'Neill. All the actions seemed scripted, as if this had happened before and we were just playing our parts. At the same time, I had no idea what would happen next.

Gabe continued to insist that I had no right to make him

leave: "I will tell the cops to arrest you for trying to kidnap me. You know I'm twenty years old, and you can't tell me what to do anymore." When the police arrived—three hefty officers—they just smiled at his claim that I was kidnapping him. "Okay, Gabe. It's your choice. We can put you in a taxi, and your dad can take you home to Chicago. Or we can check you in at Bellevue. Which will it be?"

We were in the taxi only a few minutes when Gabe burst out sobbing. "Dad, Dad," he said. "There's something inside of me, something in my head. They are screaming at me, and I can't make them stop." I held him in my arms all the way to LaGuardia. "What are the voices saying to you?" I asked. "I don't know. Hateful stuff. People just look like devils to me." When we got to the airport, we smoked cigarettes in silence and then ran for the gate.

I am told that in terms of energy per cubic millimeter, the human brain emits thirty times as much energy as an equivalent volume of the sun. This may be what I was feeling in the air that day. Years later, as I plunged into the research for Gabe's film about schizophrenia, I read the famous memoir of psychosis by Daniel Paul Schreber, with its descriptions of vivid hallucinations and "speaking rays" coming at his nerves from all sides, and immediately recalled this day. The nervous energy of Gabe's psychotic break seemed to produce a force field that enveloped both of us. Perhaps this was a particularly literal form of what Freud calls "transference," when the psychic relation between Gabe and me exploded in a crisis and was acted out in real time and space, as if we were linked by invisible wires. When he let me hold him in the taxi, I felt a surge of relief, as if a wall had been broken, some kind of truth was coming into his consciousness, and our souls had reconnected. In fact, this seemed to mark a moment when we returned to the kind of bond we had enjoyed before he left for college.

The ensuing summer of 1994 that he spent with his cousins and Aunt Patti and Uncle Mizzie turned out to be the calm before the storm. On every side I could feel the stress rising like an unstoppable flood. Janice was diagnosed with breast cancer and began undergoing treatment. Gabe was completely unsympathetic and blamed her for the illness, informing her that it was caused by drinking coffee. I was having two martinis before dinner and two cups of coffee afterward to deal with the stress of serving as chair of an ambitious, contentious English department. I began having panic attacks, the worst coming one evening at the Jazz Showcase, when I had to stumble outside in the midst of a concert to find a way to breathe. I thought I was having a heart attack. And then my beloved sister Kathleen, who had been struggling with brain cancer, was descending into the final months of her life. When I was a child, Kathleen had been my second mother while our widowed mother worked full-time to support three children on seventy-five dollars a week. Kathleen was six years older than me, the indulgent sister (Marylee, my older sister, was the strict one) who spoiled her little brother by helping him build treehouses and carrying him on her handlebars up into the foothills above Carson City. Gabe did not know how to behave at his Aunt Kathleen's funeral and was almost catatonic in the midst of what felt like the disintegration of our family. I did not know how to behave, furious that the priest at the funeral service barely spoke about my sister and used the occasion to celebrate the glory of Mother Church.

Finally, summer ended, and the long-expected breakdown occurred. One day in September 1994, Gabe exploded, kicking over chairs, shouting at us. He dashed upstairs to my study to trash my computer, and when I pursued him, he grabbed a fifteen-pound barbell and threatened to hit me with it. I tried to subdue him, but he was too strong for me, and this time I did not feel sure that he would not hurt me. Janice was yelling at both of us to stop fighting. It was as if all Dr. B's wise advice about "getting tough" with him had come to nothing but a stupid macho wrestling match. I felt completely helpless, and it stupidly crossed my mind that we should have taken Gabe up on the notion he once floated of going into the military, where a tough drill instructor could have straightened him out. "We have to call the police," Janice said. But when she went for the phone, Gabe grabbed it from her and ripped the wires out of the wall. Janice sent me to call from a neighbor's house while she calmed him down. I explained to the police dispatcher that our son was having a mental breakdown and needed to be taken to the hospital. When I got back to the house, Gabe was sitting quietly in the kitchen, drinking tea with Janice. The arrival of the cops, strangely, did not seem to surprise or upset him. He agreed to be taken to Michael Reese Hospital, where he was checked into the locked psychiatric ward.

A fierce argument about medication ensued. We were the ones who were sick, not him. We should be put away for child abuse, not him. We arranged a phone conversation with Carmen, and she convinced him to accept the medication. He insisted on one condition: that Janice should be there to witness the injection. A dose of Haldol, a powerful antipsychotic sedative, calmed him down and we began negotiations with him to continue taking medication. Since he had turned twenty-one, we were in no position to force him to take it without a court order. When we threatened to go to court, he reluctantly signed an agreement that he would accept the meds.

After two weeks, he was released into a temporary facility, a restricted floor at Chicago's historic Lawson YMCA, an urban refuge since the Great Depression, while we searched for a safe place for him to live.

A long, slow, painful rebirth began—an eighteen-year odyssey of return, loneliness, setbacks, and what looked like triumph. Gabe emerged from the hospital, redefined as schizophrenic and calmed by the Haldol that made him like a sleepwalker. "Dad," he told me, "they tell me I have a thought disorder, but I don't have any thoughts. I feel as if I'm living underwater." Gabe never had to be hospitalized again—rather unusual, since most people with schizophrenia undergo multiple hospitalizations. On the advice of our new friends at NAMI, the wonderful, indispensable National Alliance on Mental Illness, Gabe never returned home to live with us, either. It had become clear to us and the doctors we consulted that living at home was impossible for him, and at the same time he needed lots of material and spiritual support from us. We had to construct an arm's-length relationship. The goal became his gaining independence of us while still feeling secure and loved. After the transition period at the YMCA, we found a place for him at Humboldt House, a supervised residence operated by the Thresholds agency, which provided twenty-four-hour staff to administer medication and social services.

We established a routine. Janice and I talked to him on the phone almost every day and rendezvoused with him weekly at a café in Chicago's Old Town, where he hung out most days with a motley crew of students, grifters, and unemployed friends. After Mexican food at Las Piñatas (always the same trio of enchiladas mole, chiles rellenos, and the Las Piñatas Special), we would go to the movies at Piper's Alley and then drive him back to Humboldt Park. One film stands out: on the drive back to Humboldt House after seeing the premiere of Quentin Tarantino's *Pulp Fiction*, Gabe suddenly rattled off from memory the terrifying monologue performed by Samuel L. Jackson, a quote from Ezekiel 25:17:

> The path of the righteous man is beset on all sides by the inequities of the selfish and the tyranny of evil men. Blessed is he, who in the name of charity and good will, shepherds the weak through the valley of darkness, for he is truly his brother's keeper and the finder of lost children. And I will strike down upon thee with great vengeance and furious anger those who would attempt to poison and destroy my brothers. And you will know my name is the Lord when I lay my vengeance upon thee.

Gabe loved reciting this passage, and it became part of our postmovie ritual of trading speeches from films that we had just seen or—like the ubiquitous *Godfather* trilogy—knew by heart ("My father taught me many things in this room. He taught me to keep my friends close, but my enemies even closer"; "Leave the gun. Take the cannoli"). He came home often and was always with us on holidays and family trips.

So Gabe got his wish to join the homeless, but not in the way he had hoped, or we had feared. He told us more than once that we had "cast him out," and at Humboldt House he found himself immersed in the community of mental illness and addiction, living in Chicago's Humboldt Park, a neighborhood dominated by Latin street gangs. "Nice" neighborhoods don't want the mentally ill living among them. He believed (against all evidence) that the smell of crack was coming in his window from the apartment below, and his own apartment reeked from his chain-smoking. He told us that a woman on his floor had asked him to hang out at her place. When he arrived (as he told us), he found her cuddling with her girlfriend and watching porn, and she invited him to join in. Not a great environment for someone with a mental illness, we thought, and we often asked ourselves whether he should come back home to live with us. But we had no way of independently verifying his lurid stories of life at Humboldt House. Drugs and alcohol were strictly forbidden there, and infractions could result in expulsion. We also sensed that one purpose of these stories was to make us feel guilty for kicking him out and reasserting his never-abandoned view that his was the voice of reality.

The coffee shop scene in Chicago's Old Town was Gabe's refuge outside Humboldt House, but it could also be a trap. He was an easy mark for con men, who quickly tuned into his grandiose fantasies. One particular character, "Doc," claimed to have medical training. He told Gabe that there was nothing wrong with him, that his parents were leading him astray with all this crap about "mental illness." He promised Gabe a job as a model, dangling the prospect of lots of money. Doc lured Gabe into a check-kiting scheme by having him open a bank account and then deposit into it a thousand dollars' worth of Doc's checks drawn on an empty account at a Detroit bank. The next step was to use the bank's ATM card to make withdrawals, most of which Doc would keep for himself, giving Gabe just enough to make it seem like a sweet deal. When Doc's checks bounced, the shit hit the fan and the bank tried to hold us responsible for the losses. We pointed out that it was their fault for issuing an activated card before the checks had cleared. After some threatening letters, the bank finally absorbed the loss.

Doc later appeared on television when his con game made

the nightly news. Most of Gabe's new friends were harmless, and some were also homeless, like the "Mayor of Old Town," a panhandler who would greet us at the corner of North Avenue and Wells. "Here comes your wonderful mom and dad," he would say, and we routinely gave him "just enough to pay for a bed for the night."

Over the next eight years, Gabe slowly found his way through this labyrinth with the help of therapists, social workers, and the Thresholds agency. Equally crucial were the work and friendships with what are called "prosumers" (in contrast to the "consumer" model usually assigned to clients in the mental health system). Prosumers are people who have crossed the threshold into some form of health: work, service to others, the attainment of a measure of calm and optimism. Thread by thread, we constructed a safety net around him. A series of wonderful social workers monitored his behavior and kept us posted on how he was doing. A prosumer named Joe Kerouac (a distant cousin of the famous novelist), who suffered from bipolar disorder, became Gabe's mentor in helping him socialize to the mental health system. Joe also invited him to join his study group, Community Scholars, where he had to show up for classes to learn things he had missed in school, such as long division. Although to us he never completely accepted his diagnosis, within the Thresholds system he became something of a model patient, proudly displaying the certificates they awarded. In one of Gabe's films, he scans the wall of his apartment where all his awards were framed and hung.

Around 1998 he began to get involved in filmmaking and theater groups. He started taking film production classes at Columbia College and joined a filmmakers group where he began to play the role of mentor. Through Thresholds he attended a theater group called the Artistic Home, where he was introduced to the Meisner Method. That method, a spinoff of the Stanislavski Method, which emphasizes the authenticity and inner life of the actor rather than that of the character he is trying to portray, turned out to be not so good for him. When a theater game required him to slap the face of a young woman in an emotionally "authentic" scene, he walked out indignantly.

In 2002, Gabe made a big step forward. Without any help from us, he found a rental apartment in the Chicago architectural landmark, Marina City, available with a subsidy from Section 8 of Social Security's disability benefits. The cautious landlord agreed to rent to him, backed by our assurances that the rent would be paid. In this new environment outside the Thresholds system, with a view over the Chicago River on a wonderful urban landscape, he began to blossom as an outsider artist and filmmaker, writing visionary scripts (complete with storyboards), graphic novels, and poems and working on cubic grid sculptures based in speculative cosmologies. He began to move beyond the mental health community as well, developing friendships within Chicago's artistic and activist communities and immersing himself in film history and production in classes with Roger Ebert and Michael Wilmington. It had been eight years since he left NYU. He was thirty-one years old.

CHAPTER FIVE

From Desolation to Da Jewels

Thresholds had given Gabe his first real job after his entry into the world of mental illness and official disability. There was nothing glamorous about it. He had to get up at 5:00 a.m. and catch two buses to get from Humboldt Park to the Threshold offices by 7:00, where he was expected to clean toilets and mop floors—not exactly to the taste of a philosopher-king with ambitions to become a famous Hollywood director. His devoted social worker, Jill Voronoff, gave him wakeup calls to keep him on schedule, though truth be told, he would often go back to sleep.

An obsessive-compulsive scholar, I put myself to work assembling a library of madness, from the *Diagnostic and Statistical Manual of Mental Disorders* to the comforts of E. Fuller Torrey's *Surviving Schizophrenia*, and Gabe joined me in this reading program. Unsurprisingly, he was especially drawn to the antipsychiatry movement—Gilles Deleuze and Felix Guattari on "capitalism and schizophrenia" and R. D. Laing on "the divided self." Michel Foucault's *Madness and Civilization* gave us some context for the work imperative. We learned that people have always wanted to put the mentally ill to work, either as a means of moral reform, as punishment, or as therapy. During the Middle Ages, the mad were regarded as outcasts, vagabonds, mendicants, and beggars. And when we say "regarded as," it is because those were precisely the roles they filled in medieval society. There were, of course, other options: hermit, saint, martyr, witch, or professional comedian (or "licensed fool," as the mad King Lear puts it). The mad were sent away on "ships of fools," thrust out of the city, or confined to a workhouse. They filled the spaces vacated by lepers, as Foucault famously argued, without the alibi of a visible illness for their idleness, and so were whipped through the streets, branded, and treated as unrepentant sinners. The mad were those who refused to work, or could not because they were so withdrawn and catatonic that they warehoused in degrading conditions. In the eighteenth century, they were subjected to forced labor and confinement, and convenient narratives of moral improvement were combined with promises of economic productivity, which fell apart when the "working poor" depressed wages so much that they simply spread the plague of penury and homelessness. It was not until the nineteenth century that work began to be seen as therapy for sick minds, and by midcentury, this would include exposure to therapeutic arts and crafts.

In 2002, almost ten years into his illness, Gabe graduated from his work at Thresholds and landed a job as a produce clerk at the Jewel Food Store—affectionately known as "Da Jewels" by the workers and clientele. He worked at Jewel for nine years logging twenty hours per week until the fall of 2011, when he asked for a leave so that he could go back to school at Columbia College, where he started over as a thirty-eight-year-old sophomore (NYU gave him credit for his freshman year) in the documentary film program. The job gave him a routine, spending money, and self-respect. When people asked him what he did for a living, he described "Da Jewels" as his day job, with limited hours so that he could pursue his real career as a filmmaker. He developed expertise with produce and loved to bring home special offerings of exotic fruits and vegetables: persimmons, kiwi fruit, rutabaga, and the whole spectrum of herbs were his special loves. He liked to regale us with stories about what produce was picked by exploited laborers—that is, pretty much all of it. "Do you know how much they pay the people who pick those 'on the vine' tomatoes you like so much? You don't want to know."

The job could also be quite stressful. Although Gabe's supervisors had certified proof of his diagnosis as a disabled person and his need to work limited hours, he was continually under pressure to work extra hours and to fill in when other employees failed to show up. This created problems with his Social Security disability benefits when he worked more than the allowed quota of hours. SSA disability benefits come with a catch-22: success is penalized by a cut in benefits. If you work one hour more than your assigned quota for the month, you may be required to repay the government the entire amount of your monthly benefit. Despite our reassurances to Gabe that we would deal with the demands from Social Security, he was deeply disturbed by the cascade of computer-generated bills that were coming to him in the mail, accompanied by threatening language about the severe penalties for non-payment. When Janice, as "representative payee," talked to actual people at Social Security about the situation, they were invariably sympathetic and reassuring, but the bureaucratic machinery continued to crank out the alarming notices that filled Gabe's mailbox. This reached a crisis when, two years after Gabe's death, the SSA computers cranked out a bill for $46,981.90 of "excess benefits" over several years. Gabe's absence from the world without a will settled the whole matter for good.

Gabe's punctuality and his excellent personal grooming made his disability invisible to most people, including his supervisors at Jewel. The more successful his adaptation to stressful work conditions, the more store management was tempted to pile on more stress. Gabe often worked late hours at night and then would be ordered to arrive early (6:00 a.m.) the next morning. His sleep, always vulnerable to insomnia and nightmares, was affected severely by these demands, and no amount of explaining to his supervisors (or invocation of union rules) seemed to make a difference. He was constantly anxious about being fired and complained about the routine humiliations and casual cruelty of an hourly working-class job, of which (he loved to remind us) we had little or no experience. When he made the mistake of sharing his dreams of success as a filmmaker with his coworkers, his ambitions were ridiculed: "Are you polishing up your Oscar yet?" He told us that one of his supervisors, annoyed at Gabe's reminders about his disability status and his reluctance to work extra hours, told him he was just a spoiled rich kid who might need to be straightened out by some of his mobster friends if he kept complaining. Was this just a joke to needle the young guy who dressed too well to be a grocery clerk? We never found out.

I often wondered whether I could have put up with these

conditions after so many years of enjoying the cushy life of an academic, setting my own hours and teaching smart kids at an elite university. I had worked my way through college with unpleasant jobs, tearing down buildings for ten dollars per twelve-hour day and washing dishes in a fast food restaurant. But these were temporary summer jobs, nothing like the endless grind that Gabe was enduring. When I offered to go to Gabe's supervisor and explain the situation, he refused indignantly, declaring that this would just make his life there more miserable. "Don't you dare!" he said. The idea of having "Daddy" intervene on his behalf was intolerable to him. I had to respect his wishes about this and restrain myself from dropping into "Da Jewels" to confront management about their treatment of my son. Because Gabe presented himself so well, it was easy for them to forget that he had a mental illness. "You don't look disabled to me" was the refrain of his supervisors.

Nevertheless, he was proud of being a produce man and liked to flaunt his skillful eye for the "luggage" in our own refrigerator that needed to go into the garbage. He learned to operate a forklift and would brag about his John Henry–like speed records in moving half-ton pallets of potatoes. He visited the central distribution warehouse, an enormous facility where all the groceries for the city of Chicago would arrive every night to be trucked all over the city by daybreak. He was good with customers and had an especial knack for dealing with elderly ladies' complaints about the quality of the produce. He performed vivid impressions of typical dialogues in his best old-lady voice: "Young man! Are these the best cherries you have? They look overripe to me." To which he would say, "Yes, ma'am! I will have a look in the back and see if we have something better." He would then bring out a box of cherries that were, of course, from the same batch as the ones on display and offer those to the customer. "Well, that's more like it. Aren't these much, much better? You should throw out those other ones." When some of these ladies found out his name was Gabriel, and that his mother and grandmother were Jewish, they adopted him as their personal guardian angel of produce. It wasn't long before Gabe won an award for Best Customer Relations in the entire Chicago-area Jewel food chain. And a day came when he was asked if he would like to move up to a salaried management position. He turned this down on the very reasonable grounds that the long hours would mean the end of his benefits and the prospects for his artistic career; and he was wisely aware that the added responsibility would be very stressful and might cause even more extreme flare-ups of the mental illness that was his constant companion.

Gabe's favorite supervisor at the Uptown Jewel was Bob Johnson, an older man who taught him the craft of produce and nicknamed Gabe his "Home Skillet," a term of endearment that he adopted as his moniker on his website's "mission statement": "With his beard in hand, and an unrequited lust for adventure, the Skillet is homeward bound." Bob was a lifer in the produce business and an institution at Jewel. He took Gabe under his wing, and when Gabe started making video interviews with his friends and acquaintances as well as the homeless, he asked Bob to tell him his philosophy of life. Bob's answer: "My philosophy? As you go through life, no matter how well things are going, just remember that there is always someone waiting to cut off your head and stick it up your butt!" Bob liked the way Gabe interacted with the annoying customers he could spot a mile off. When Bob saw some difficult ladies heading into produce, he would beat a retreat into the back rooms. "Skillet," he would say, "I see the Soul Sistahs coming. You handle it. I'm going for a smoke."

It was no surprise, then, when Gabe began thinking about making a film entitled *Da Jewels*, in which he planned to combine a documentary of a day in the life of a big-city grocery store with a heist film about a multimillion-dollar jewel theft. The full script was never written, as far as I know, but we talked about it many times. The aim of the film would be to turn his daily life into a madcap festival or carnival, a comic-action film modeled on the 1963 classic *It's a Mad, Mad, Mad, Mad World*.

Da Jewels was to feature a high-speed cops-and-robbers car chase through Chicago inspired by *The Blues Brothers* and a scattering of jewels along the route of the Gay Pride Parade. In Gabe's film, the diamonds would have been hidden inside hundreds of watermelons supplied by Jewel, and the bursting of watermelons and the scattering of real diamonds on the streets was to incite a climactic crowd scene crosscut with the frantic car chase to city hall.

But my favorite scene from *Da Jewels* was Gabe's vision of the opening credits. Here is how he described it in screenwriters' format:

INTERIOR OF UPTOWN JEWEL FOOD STORE: 3:00 AM
The store brightly lit and the PA system blasting out Rage Against the Machine while stock boys wearing rollerblades zoom through the aisles restocking the shelves. Hundreds of cameras are mounted at numerous angles in the style of Lars von Trier's *Dancer in the Dark*, with the main action filmed at floor level by a camera on a skateboard ridden by the director, racing through the aisles tracking the rollerbladers. This continues while the opening credits roll, ending in a climac-

tic shot as the music ends in a quiet back room with masked figures huddled around a stack of watermelons. A deep baritone voiceover introduces the film as a documentary of a day in the life of an urban supermarket. "A lot goes on behind the scenes in a big-city grocery store that customers know very little about . . ." And thus Act 1 begins, with closeups of glittering diamonds being inserted into the watermelons.

Da Jewels was Gabe's way of turning his work, and his workplace, from a place of drudgery, business, or therapy into a space of play and improvisation. The screenplay reimagines this ordinary commercial space as the site of anarchy and the ancient form of madness that is cultivated deliberately as part of a communal practice, a shared delusion. Plato called it "initiatory" madness and connected it with Dionysian ritual—in short, with festival, carnival, and mass hysteria. Instead of using work as a therapy for madness, Gabe put madness to work on work itself. It was as if he wanted to overcome Foucault's axiom: "madness, or the absence of the work."

Many of the residents of Humboldt House were very inactive, spending their days sitting around smoking. Gabe was getting out, using his bit of Spanish to mix with the local Hispanic gangbangers, the Vice Lords. He told us about hair-raising gang fights in which gunfire echoed across the turf border of Humboldt Boulevard between the Latin Kings and the Gangster Disciples. He was proud of the pastel portrait that he used on his business card, claiming that he had paid a junkie ten dollars to make it. And he bragged shamelessly about his street smarts, telling everyone about a special favor offered to him by one of his gangbanger neighbors: "Hey, amigo. You are all right. Just let me know if you want anybody killed. I do it for you for free."

FIGURE 7. Gabe's portrait, "Gabe's 'junkie' business card" (n.d.).

All the while that Gabe was making such steady progress, gaining increased mastery as a filmmaker and expanding his horizons, he was accompanied by the disturbing forces of his illness, which often burst out in episodes of anger, depression, and frustration. His obsession with Cricket never completely went away, resurfacing at moments of stress. And we knew that right alongside his rebirth as a charming young man, smart, honest, kind, and gentle, he was still fighting with— and trying to protect his parents from knowing about—his world of auditory hallucinations and nightmares. Any of us might be annoyed by passing thoughts about our own short-comings; for Gabe, these were amplified into a tormenting cacophony of sneering, self-destructive voices. "Kill the bald eagle! Kill the bald eagle!" was the refrain shouted at him by the voices in his head. When I asked him, "Who is the bald eagle, Gabe?" he responded, "It's me, of course." And it did not escape my notice that *Crazy Talk* was framed by *Vanilla Sky*'s images of Tom Cruise's suicidal plunge from the top of a skyscraper. Even as Gabe matured into a handsome young man, the shadow of schizophrenia would sometimes pass over his face.

On June 24, 2012, I was at a White Sox game with friends. Gabe had called that morning to say that he didn't feel like coming. I received a text message from Janice: "Problem with Gabe. Come home." The bike ride back to Hyde Park seemed endless, like one of those nightmares where you are running on a treadmill. When I reached home a few minutes later, my worst nightmare became a horrible reality. Janice knew what had happened the minute she saw the policeman at our front door. "A man fell from the west tower of Marina City a few hours ago. He has been identified as your son, Gabriel." Gabe had evidently jumped from the balcony of his apartment on the fifty-ninth floor. What did we do next? The day is complete chaos in my memory. Did we go to the morgue? Or rush downtown to see if it was all a mistake? The most vivid recollection I have is entering his apartment and finding everything in order, the dishes washed, the bed made, his drafting tools neatly assembled on his drafting table, his laptop open, laden with recent emails from and to fellow filmmakers who wanted to work with him. The only strange detail was his Zyprexa pill bottles, along with the printouts describing side effects, on the kitchen counter next to an empty pack of cigarettes. It seemed obvious to us that he did not plan his suicide, even though in retrospect it has come to seem inevitable. An obsessive communicator, he did not leave a note. Was he driven over the edge, like the falling men and women of 9/11, by the intolerable flames inside his head? Did a tsunami of voices sweep him away?

CHAPTER SIX

Flying & Falling

In the days after Gabe's death, immersed in a whirlwind of
friends and family, a blur of voices and faces in which it
seemed like everyone I have ever loved was converging on
us, I felt the ghosts of Grandpa Rocco, Grammy Florence, and
Grandma Leona swirling around us, and somehow expected
them to walk in the door with Carmen, and my living sisters
Sandra Ryan and Marylee Tyler accompanied by Kathleen,
gone from life for almost twenty years. Amid the turmoil was
the quiet presence of our next-door neighbor Bill Ayers, pick-
ing up people at the airport, making meals for us, and then
discreetly withdrawing despite our pleas for him to join us:
"You don't need me around. You need to be with your family."

But the word I recall being repeated endlessly, like a tolling
bell in those days, is "unimaginable." I have often wondered
why people always say that the death of a child is unimag-

inable—"I can't imagine what you are going through" is the routine expression of sympathy. My sense is just the opposite. It is all too imaginable. It may be one of the primary foundations of imagination, especially when driven by all the fears that are built into the parenting of any child, let alone one who seems especially vulnerable. Is the "can't imagine" really a cruel way to distance oneself from the tragedy, in other words, to say it can't happen to me, a refusal of empathy masquerading as consolation? Or is it affirmation by denial—of saying, I can all-too-vividly imagine what it is like to lose a child, and therefore I have to shut down my imagination and respect the reality and singularity of your grief? Either way, it is what people say.

My first premonition of the manner of Gabe's death was in his early childhood, a recurrent dream as he began to enter the toddler phase, walking, climbing, and (inevitably) putting himself at risk. My nightmare always had the same structure: Gabe has climbed out of his crib and is crawling toward his bedroom window on the front of the house. He has opened the screen and crawled out on the porch roof. He is crawling toward the edge, and I come scrambling out the window to grab him by the heel just as he goes over the edge. I can feel his pudgy little ankle secure in my grip, and then I wake up with a start.

Out the window, through the window, through the looking glass. I see Gabe putting his hand through our kitchen window to "reality test" his teasing Grandpa Rocco; sitting for long stretches gazing out the front window of our house; falling past the windows of a skyscraper in *Vanilla Sky* or the opening credits of *Mad Men*, the TV series about the craziness of the advertising industry; rhapsodizing about flying with his skateboard over the "hips" of Chicago's curbs; flying off the back porch to break his foot, or leaping from the landing on our front stairs to land in my arms; throwing his camera off the roof of Marina Towers; soaring with his favorite gravity-defying superheroes.

When Gabe moved into Marina City, I was strangely oblivious to the presence of the imminent danger right outside his door. Every apartment in Marina City has a spacious balcony with a steel railing about five feet high. So easy to look straight down the fifty-nine stories to the street far below. So easy to lean one's head over the railing and imagine the fall. So easy to climb over the railing and do what one has just imagined with a thrill of fear and excitement.

I have always loved high places, and I loved hanging out on Gabe's balcony, high above the Chicago River. Looking down and imagining the fall is for me an intoxicating mixture of delight and terror. I immediately think of flying, and my own dreams have always been of flying. Sometimes I dream of flying over the countryside pursued by a witch on a broomstick. I am much faster than her, however, so I fly in circles around her and leave her in the distance. But she is persistent and steady. She keeps coming over the horizon, and slowly I begin to lose my power of flight. The ability of my outstretched arms to hold me aloft starts to wane, and as I settle to earth, I see her still coming and I wake up.

Janice was much more aware of the danger of Marina City than I was. She demanded from the first that he reassure us that he would never jump. He was emphatic about it. "I would never do anything like that. What do you think? That I'm stupid or crazy? No way could I do that."

But he did, and of course we should have seen it coming. I especially should have been more alert, more imaginative. But I laughed off the possibility the way I laughed it off when he was a toddler and drank muddy rainwater from the gutter in the street in front of our house. Janice was alarmed: "You did what?" Then to me: "Should we force him to throw up or rush him to the emergency room?" I chose to treat this as Gabe's mischievous tormenting of his mother's imagination. So I tried to calm Janice down, saying loud enough for Gabe to hear: "I'm sure he wouldn't do that. He is a smart boy. He's not stupid or crazy enough to drink filthy water out of the gutter." I caught Gabe's eye and winked at him, receiving what I took to be a wink of recognition in return. ("No. In fact, he did drink it" is the note Janice wrote in the margin on this page in typescript.)

Since Gabe's death, I have been unable to go very many days without imagining his last moments. It is a kind of waking dream, a horror film in slow motion. I see him hanging up the phone after our last conversation, in which he angrily accused me of never having read his film scripts. He smokes a cigarette and pulls out his bottles of Zyprexa to read the fine print about side effects. The voices are pounding in his head like a surf or a firestorm, and his stereo cannot drown them out. He paces up and down, filled with movie memories of Tom Cruise diving from an office building and awakening into a different reality in *Vanilla Sky*. He puts his cigarettes and wallet down, takes off his glasses, and goes to the railing. In a talk about his film *Crazy Talk*, he had expressed a wish to film the experience of falling by throwing his camera over the edge of the roof of Marina Towers. (He decided not to do this for the obvious reason that the camera would be destroyed, along with the desired footage. "I would need special equipment for that.") In his final moments, was he his own camera, his own special equipment, taking the place of Tom Cruise in *Vanilla Sky*? He looks over the edge, climbs over the railing, balances himself there for a moment with his back to the street. He lets go and falls backward fifty-nine stories.

When I replay this film in my head, a constructed memory of something I have never seen, I try to shake off the horrid daydream. I try to run the film back to our phone conversation on June 24, 2012, and start over by insisting that I have read his screenplays, and I am coming downtown to spend the day with him. I see myself opening the door of his apartment just as he is climbing over the railing. I run to the balcony and catch him by his wrists just as he is letting go. But he is too heavy for me to hold, and I find myself falling with him. He is falling; we are falling. He has fallen forever.

CHAPTER SEVEN

Diagnoses & Detours

Gabe was in many ways the typical subject of psychiatry from the 1980s forward. He was diagnosed with depression at age 13 but seemed to pull out of that condition with tactics of rebelliousness. Janice and I comforted ourselves with the usual narrative: "It's just a phase." He and his friends organized a "Bad Boys Club" at the University of Chicago's elite Laboratory School. They smoked pot on the grounds, short-circuited the school's electrical system with well-placed hairpins, and generally failed to conform.

Gabe was politely encouraged to leave the Lab School shortly after he took time away to go with me on a lecture trip to Israel in November of 1987, where we arrived during the onset of the first Palestinian uprising, the "Children's Intifada," as it was then known. I spoke at a conference on landscape at Bar-Ilan University, a slide lecture that examined patterns of settlement architecture in the West Bank, and connected Zi-onism with colonialism. Gabe had the rare pleasure of watch-ing his father caught in the crossfire of Israel's internal de-bates. On the one side, I was accused of being a communist and dangerous Palestinian sympathizer; on the other, I was defended for saying and showing what many liberal Israelis already knew. Gabe seemed to enjoy all of this immensely, and I felt like it was the first time he had a glimpse of what his dad did for a living. "Why are they all attacking you, Dad? Doesn't it bother you?"

It was a magical moment in my relationship with him. He was a buoyant, gregarious thirteen-year-old, suddenly im-mersed in a world where, in Israeli culture, to be a Jewish boy at the Bar Mitzvah age of thirteen and called "Gabriel" is to be treated like an angel (and to behave like a smart-aleck devil) with all sorts of indulgences ("Dad promised to bring me to the holy land, but where are all the holes?") Plus, Janice's best friend Judy, an American émigrée to Israel, and her Sephardic husband, Bennie, had a son—a boy named Gavriel ("Gavri"), exactly the same age as Gabe. The five of us traveled all over Israel together, from Eilat to Galilee with our two angels/dev-ils in a small car. During a nighttime pit stop on the side of the road to the Galilee, Gavri outraged his mother—and de-lighted his honorary cousin—by standing on the side of the road and launching a heroic arc of urine into the headlights of the oncoming cars, which honked their appreciation at his audacity. Judy insisted that Bennie stop laughing and admin-ister punishment, so Gavri was rewarded by a completely in-effectual smack on the side of his head.

We went on to visit Masada, the boys giggling in the back seat, where we listened to the solemn lesson by the tour guide, one that has been repeated thousands of times. Masada, the mountaintop fortress where a few hundred Hebrew Zealots held out from 66 to 73 CE against the Roman legions and then committed mass suicide rather than be taken prisoner, is, we were told, an allegory of modern Israel. The lesson is that the next time Israel is threatened by external enemies, it will not commit suicide alone, but (thanks to nuclear weapons) will take the rest of the world along with it. While this homily was being recited, our two angels/devils were folding the Masada brochures into paper airplanes and flying them off the cliff down toward the ruins of the Roman fort.

After the Lab School asked him to leave, Gabe seemed happy to transfer to the nearby public Kenwood High School. On the day I took him to Kenwood High to register, two girls he knew happened to be in the office. "Hey, Gabe," one said. "What are you doing here? Are you coming to Kenwood?" When he nodded yes, one of them said, "Whoa. That is so cool. Would you like to hang out with us?"

Gabe quickly made friends, smoked pot, raided our liquor cabinet, and skateboarded with the "Wiggers," the white boys who adopted hip-hop culture, tagged underpasses with graffiti, and identified with the black kids. He was arrested for urinating under the El tracks and had his ears boxed by a Chicago cop. When I went to the station to pick him up, I complained to the desk sergeant about the injury. The sergeant gave me a contemptuous smirk and told me that if I would like to file a complaint, the police would be happy to revisit the charge of disorderly conduct and raise it to resisting arrest. With Gabe's ears still ringing from the beating, I quietly retreated and took him home.

Janice and I thought of him as a typical unruly teenager with a healthy rebellious streak and a growing fund of street cred. Our family legends of encounters with police at antiwar rallies in the 1960s probably reinforced his sense that the road of anarchism and excess led directly to Blake's Palace of Wisdom. One could make a case (and I have accused myself of this many times) that we were irresponsible and should have exerted more control over him. Later, with the support of Dr. B, Gabe would accuse us of having failed to discipline him sufficiently, to help form his character and destiny. "You just let me do whatever I wanted, didn't you? And now look at the mess you have made."

This is also the time he would recall later in new explanations of his illness as one of trauma and betrayal. Displacing his tale of unrequited love with Cricket, he developed an elaborate narrative of being hit on the head with a tire iron, perhaps by his own comrades, during a confrontation with a street gang. Beyond a constant case of "road rash" and scrapes from skateboarding, we did not notice any evidence of traumatic events of this sort, certainly not the twenty-four comatose hours he wanted us to recall. Memories of this sort would later become major points of contention in our effort to figure out what was ailing him. Recovered memories of this trauma became his way of claiming that his illness was not schizophrenia but post-traumatic stress disorder (PTSD), a diagnosis that he preferred because it allowed him to blame his friends as traitors and accuse his parents of neglect and abandonment. It was also more acceptable socially and seemed to be everywhere as soldiers from our wars in Iraq and Afghanistan were coming home with it, providing him with vivid newspaper headlines about the epidemic of mental illness to insert into the montage of *Crazy Talk*. Above all, it helped him to replace the Cricket narrative with a brain injury, a way of pushing it away from his interior, his mind, soul, and identity toward outer circumstances. He was using physiological, traumatic explanations of his illness to talk his way out of a broken heart, replacing it with a broken head.

We went to a series of therapists who tried out labels from "immaturity aggravated by weak parenting" (Dr. B), "manic depression," "borderline personality disorder," and "learning disability" to "schizotypal" and "schizophrenic." "Thought disorder" (Dr. L) seemed to be the most general term, accompanied by paranoia and auditory hallucinations. The decisive moment of hospitalization in 1994 could not have come at a worse time. The ensuing period—the Haldol days—were deeply depressing for all of us. We all felt like we were living underwater with him.

What is there to say about these diagnoses? With each label comes a stereotypical case history, a "disease picture" that fulfills all the generic requirements of a specific form of mental illness. The label becomes a prospective destiny, a fatal screen or grid through which one sees the individual. Madness is not so much a matter of seeing something definite out there in the world as it is a matter of "seeing as"— which implies hearing, describing, and narrating—the whole discourse of labels and behaviors. We greeted each diagnosis with deeply mixed feelings: Is this finally it? Have we gotten to the bottom of it? Which passages in the *Diagnostic and Statistical Manual of Mental Disorders* (*DSM*) can tell us what to expect? Which ones tell us what to do? The naming of the illnesses seemed to have a kind of temporary palliative effect, as if the label somehow gave us control. Our life seemed to spiral inward, and our social life became increasingly narrow, restricted to a few friends and relatives, even as our professional lives were expanding.

CHAPTER EIGHT

"He Killed the Future"

These were the first articulate words I uttered on the day of Gabe's death as Janice and I hugged and wept. They were preceded by plenty of inarticulate sounds, but they summed up the core of my grief. What future? Whose future? His, of course, but also mine, Janice's, Carmen's. There had been profound changes in the father-son relationship that we both cherished, despite all the negativity of my role as the "reality principle" for him, and that had given me a picture of the future that may be unusual in the parent of an adult child. The fact is, Gabe had long since made the transition from being my son to being my best friend. We shared so much. Idolization of Michael Jordan, whose exploits we followed religiously. Endless jokes and games, usually involving movies. Stupid clichés and quotations from Woody Allen films: "I don't wish to be facetious or didactic" was our favorite turning line in a conversation, along with "May I interject something at this juncture?"

We invented a game that involved quoting a line from a film, not with the aim—far too easy—of identifying it, but of continuing the dialogue. For example: "If you are Federales, show us your badges." For which the correct answer, of course, is "Badges? We don't need no filthy stinking badges." And this exchange would then mutate into witty ripostes occasioned by the lighting of a cigarette: "Hey, Gabe. Do you have any matches on you?" "Matches? I don't need no filthy stinking matches!" The exchanges could even crop up in the middle of a debate about his recovered memories of which Janice and I had no memory and break up the tension by casting me as Tom Cruise and Gabe as Jack Nicholson in *A Few Good Men*. "All I'm looking for, Gabe, is the truth." "The truth? The truth? You can't handle the truth!" A glum and tension-filled silence could be instantly shattered with laughter. If I was trying to draw Gabe out in my lame attempts at psychotherapy, he might ask, "So, Dr. No-No, do you expect me to talk?" To which the right answer was "No, Mr. Bond. I expect you to die!" Or we would simply insert ourselves into a patch of movie dialogue, as when I would say to him (recalling *Sunset Boulevard*), "Wait. Don't I know you? You're Gabriel Mitchell. You used to be big." And he of course would answer, "I *am* big; it's the pictures that got small."

Best of all was Gabe's skill at recasting everyday situations as scenes from movies. He liked to stage one-sided conversations with our smart little German shepherd, C.C., who was very clever at opening the cabinet door under the sink to pull out the garbage, leaving her relatively stupid Labrador companion, Lucy, to take the blame. Gabe would order C.C. to sit, then command the perplexed dog, "Talk, Schweinhund, talk!" followed by the warning: "You know, meine Schatze, zat ve have vays of makink you talk!" Gabe would almost invariably win the movie games as he immersed himself in film courses at the University of Chicago's downtown campus. He took courses on Hitchcock and Almodóvar, Buñuel and Scorsese, Kubrick and the Coen brothers, among many others. But even more important than the change from number-one son to best friend had been a momentary but momentous transformation in our respective roles as caregiver and patient. In the winter of 2010, I suffered a back injury and was confined to a wheelchair for about six weeks. Gabe looked after me, driving me to school and wheeling me to the classroom for my large lecture course in media theory. He would stay for the lectures, which I would deliver from my wheelchair, and we would talk about them as he drove me home.

He enjoyed the reversal of roles. "Careful, Dad. Don't try to lift that." He liked playing the "reality principle" for real: "Go take a rest. I'll walk the dogs." It made him feel responsible (which he was) and strong. He was incredibly considerate and affectionate. And it made me feel good, too. I liked leaning on him and bragging to everyone that "my son is strong like bull." And the reversal was more than just physical. He became my consigliere, my spiritual adviser. When we took a road trip together to visit Frank Lloyd Wright's Fallingwater in Western Pennsylvania, he took the occasion to counsel me about my own life. I had been depressed, complaining about growing old, coming to the end of my career. He pointed out to me that Wright designed Fallingwater at exactly my age (around seventy) and that his real career was just beginning. "The same applies to you, Dad. You are not at the end, but just at the threshold of your best accomplishments." I considered the possibility of retiring from the University of Chicago and starting a film production company with him. If only! At moments like that, I took a secret delight in thinking how lucky I was to have a son who had stayed so close to me well into his maturity, when everyone else had children whose lives had taken them away into successful careers in distant places. A silver lining whose comforts I kept deep inside for a future day when he would be looking after me.

I don't know if he was right in his optimism about me. But I know that when he said those kinds of things I felt completely convinced that he himself was on the threshold of achieving something extraordinary, something commensurate with his grandiose dreams and ambitions. In the last six months of his life, while continuing his job at Da Jewels, he went back to school full-time, brushing off our concerns that he was trying to do too much. His dogged persistence in mastering digital editing was paying off with the rapid production of new films, including a wonderful mash-up of scenes from Chicago in 1968 with the voice-over of Bill Ayers reading aloud from his memoir, *Fugitive Days*.

Watching his work flower, seeing him connecting with people in the "straight" world, and in the not-so-straight worlds of theater, poetry, music, film, and political activism outside the mental health system, I thought he had defeated schizophrenia and incautiously told him so. *Crazy Talk* struck me as a miniature gem in its effort to "show madness from inside and outside." I made it the introduction to a lecture, "Seeing Madness," that I took on the road in 2011 and presented as the opening chapter of the "atlas of madness" that he had commissioned from me as background for the encyclopedic *Histoire de la folie* he was planning. As Gabe began to affirm his version of "Mad Pride" and come out as an activist for the disabled and mentally ill, I felt myself swept up in his ambitions. "Stop thinking of yourself as the 'sick boy,'" I told him. "You are on the road to fulfilling all your hopes and dreams." I tried to banish the word "grandiosity" from my conversations with him and instead entered into the impossibly grand project for which he had recruited me. Strangely, I can't remember anything he said in response to my new optimism. All I can recall is a quiet smile and a shrug, his usual shorthand for telling me to get real.

Did I overdo this? Could my optimism have contributed to his feeling that he could cut down on his doses of antipsychotic medication? He hated the meds for their soporific effects and wanted to be at his best, present and alert. His idea for the blockbuster heist-documentary-comedy, *Da Jewels*, had drawn interest from one of his successful filmmaker friends, Prashant Bhargava, and we knew he wanted to be at the top of his game in preparing a treatment for the film. But this may have led him toward an "Everest moment," a disastrous encounter well known in struggles with schizophrenia. That is, the feeling that he was conquering the disease might have led him to let down his guard, to taper off on the meds. Schizophrenia was waiting like a demon for a moment of weakness when it could lure him over the edge to his final fall.

Gabe had treated images of flying and falling as the framing action of *Crazy Talk*. The film opens with a closeup of himself as a blank, staring somnambulist, his handheld camera turned to face him as he walks blindly toward the edge of the Marina Towers rooftop, accompanied by the wailing and keening sounds of Janice's choral setting to William Blake's *Mad Song*—"The light doth seize my brain with frantic pain. . . ." As he reaches the edge of the roof, the camera turns toward the view of the Chicago skyline, then suddenly cuts to a trio of spread-eagle Christ figures: a bare-chested Jim Morrison,

Mel Gibson's crucified Jesus, and Michael Jordan's "Wings" poster (captioned by Blake's proverb "No bird flies too high if it flies with its own wings"), all interpolated into the continuous shot of Tom Cruise's spread-eagle leap from a skyscraper at the end of *Vanilla Sky*. Cruise's suicidal plunge releases him from his dream state in a cryogenic incubator and allows him to "open his eyes" in the real world. At the first public screening of *Crazy Talk*, in the "Seeing Madness" seminar, one of the students asked Gabe about the significance of these figures. He responded that they were symbols of both "comfort and dismay"—the dismay of suicide and the comfort at being in the company of these heroic "friends."

Whether he did it to escape the agony of tormenting voices, or out of a hope that he would awaken in another dimension (the *Vanilla Sky* scenario), we will never know. We do know now that in the fall of 2011, while he outwardly seemed to be on the verge of defeating schizophrenia, he was writing deranged letters to the goddess of his cinematic idolatry, Cameron Diaz. In *Crazy Talk*, he cuts from a montage of newspaper headlines about mental illness among children, soldiers, and serial killers to the face of Diaz, his voice-over trembling with emotion. His final thoughts and feelings could have been either hope or despair, a fantasy of flight or a leap into oblivion. For us, no comfort. Only dismay.

CHAPTER NINE

He Was Too Strong for His Own Good

One of the common features of schizophrenia in gifted individuals is a belief that the illness can be conquered with strength of will. The portrayal of the mathematician John Nash in the film *A Beautiful Mind* exemplifies this notion, treating Nash's "recovery" from madness as a simple matter of deciding not to believe in the reality of his own hallucinations. He tells his imaginary friends to go away, and they fade into the background. A more nuanced account is provided by Elyn Saks in her autobiography, *The Center Cannot Hold.* The most important delusion that Saks has to overcome is her feeling that she can simply reason her way out of her condition: "I thought that if I could figure it out, I could conquer it. My problem was not that I was crazy; it was that I was weak" (167).

It is the oldest cliché of psychology. Denial that one has a problem is the first and hardest problem to overcome. Like the Protestant doctrine of "conviction of sin," the acknowledgment of one's own sinfulness and need for grace, the acceptance of a diagnosis or, at a minimum, the acceptance that one *needs* a diagnosis, that there is a problem in one's life that cannot be wished or willed away, is a precondition for successful treatment. And "success" can be a very complex matter, since the idea of normality and mental health is at least as vague and contradictory as the idea of madness. In the case of schizophrenia, sometimes the best notion of success is to accept one's condition as *incurable but treatable and survivable.* When Saks accepted that she would need to be continuously alert to stress, vigilant to spotting warning signs and situations (e.g., the moment of changing therapists), her life became a matter of managing schizophrenia rather than of overcoming it. When she understood that the need for medication would probably never go away, she was well on the road to what would count as a successful life. When Aby Warburg, the German historian of art and culture, emerged from his five-year confinement in a mental hospital, he defined his own condition as that of a "revenant" or ghost, an "incurable" who had found a way back into the world for an afterlife. When Judge Schreber, the mad jurist who served as the most famous exemplar of schizophrenia in modern Europe, fought to be released from his confinement, it was his writing and legal reasoning that did the trick; his elaborate system of delusions survived intact and became the mythic core for the most famous first-person account of madness in the twentieth century.

Gabriel was too strong for his own good. His therapists all testified to his ability to "present well," as the jargon puts it. He did not fit the stereotypical image of schizophrenia as

withdrawn, angry, delusional, obsessive, and all-around difficult. He saved that mostly for us. His personal grooming was
excellent. He defied the tendency of medications to induce
obesity by working out energetically, cycling, skateboarding,
stair climbing, and going to the gym. His apartment was generally quite neat, with books, tapes, and DVDs arranged log-
ically. His desk was carefully ordered with drafting tools and
materials ready to hand. Of course, the whole space always
reeked of tobacco, the most widely used self-medication for
schizophrenia.

Being a social butterfly is not part of the stereotype of
schizophrenia. At art openings, house parties, and recep-
tions, Gabe would work the room like a skilled politician,
meeting new people and engaging them in conversation and
handing out his business cards. There was not a trace of cyn-
icism or opportunism in this behavior. Live encounters with
the faces and voices of others helped to push away the de-
structive inner voices that plagued him. In spite of his empa-
thetic, sociable nature, however, he felt terribly alone in the
world and complained bitterly when people failed to show up
for appointments or canceled at the last minute. Probably they
were oblivious to the hurt they were inflicting. After his death,
scores of people came forward and testified about memora-
ble encounters with him in which they glimpsed his empathy and sensitivity (the most frequent adjectives that come
up in these anecdotes are "sweetness," "enthusiasm," "bril-
liance," and "openness"). One of his dear friends who suffered from depression remarked about a day with him: "Our
conversation made a before and after of that day for me. Afterward, we determined that our respective insurance com-
panies should pay us for providing each other with therapy,
and we also determined that I needed to get dance shoes." He

could segue from small talk to the meaning of life without missing a beat.

Many people who knew Gabe were completely unaware that he had a mental illness, and his darkest episodes were mostly confined to intimate family situations, where his anger and despair and grandiosity could flourish openly. But even within the family, he tended to conceal the depth of his suffering. When I asked about how he was feeling, I was generally rebuffed with the retort "How are *you* feeling?" When I would ask if he was having nightmares, he would often turn the question aside or, conversely, assert that they were stronger than ever, and then to go on to describe nightly dreams of being torn apart and devoured by insects, visions worthy of Bosch's lurid portrayals of the torments of hell.

I think he was engaged in a double defense mechanism: defending himself against having to open up the Pandora's box full of demons that were plaguing him, while also defending us against the intensity of his pain and reassuring us that all was well. He consistently refused to engage in serious talk therapy, even after he had come reluctantly to accept the need for medication. He preferred the passive "Rogerian" style of therapy, in which he could filibuster for the entire hour without being challenged by the therapist, whose only role was to periodically murmur "mm-hmm." And he expressed mixed feelings about this technique, sometimes mocking it quite savagely by imitating the bland clichés of professional "concern" ("And how are you feeling today?" "And how did you feel about that?"). At other times, he was willing to admit that it might be of limited benefit, and he had no problem with talking about himself. When he was asked if he ever had thoughts about suicide, he emphatically denied it, assuring us and his doctors that he would never do anything like that.

At the same time, his screenplays were projecting images of himself both as a superhero capable of amazing feats of intellectual and physical strength, and as the victim of dark forces, betrayal, and persecution. In one screenplay, *The Politics of Dreams*, he divided the character of his alter egos in two. On one side is Abby, a famous Hollywood director and actor who is about to receive an Academy Award for lifetime achievement; at the same time, he is completing his magnum opus, *Quantum Geometrics: A Unified Physics of Peace*. On the other is George, a failed screenwriter who is "a paranoid, delusional psychotic" and a drug fiend. George hates Abby for his success and for his bad taste in films. He is outraged that Abby regards *Casablanca* as a better film than *Citizen Kane*. Abby represents the "industrial" model of cinema as mass culture, while George is portrayed as the frustrated *auteur* who identifies with Orson Welles. If Abby is a projection of Gabe's grandiose ambitions, George is a portrayal of his actual suffering, beset by hideous nightmares and voices urging him to commit suicide. George tries to assassinate Abby as he walks the red carpet at the Oscars, succeeding in leaving Abby in a coma.

The interesting plot twist in *The Politics of Dreams* occurs when Abby awakens from his coma, decides to forgive his assassin, and invites him to spend time with him in his hospital room. George is brought in wearing a straitjacket, and together they watch a retrospective of all the films in Abby's long career. The films comprise every genre known to Hollywood—western, science fiction, noir, psychological thriller, courtroom drama, boxing, dinosaurs, crime procedural, war, even a picaresque biker film modeled on *Easy Rider*. Every film has a "Hollywood ending," with Abby as a cowboy, astronaut, detective, scientist, or Christ figure who always gets the girl and saves the world. George is completely contemptuous of Abby's success, insisting that these formulaic films are trashy productions for the commercial culture industry. He then reveals that he himself is a screenwriter—"My scripts are about real things, not some dream factory"—and gets a lecture from Abby on how to pander to audiences to have a successful film career.

While this retrospective is unfolding, George is busy wriggling his way out of his straitjacket so that he can finish Abby off. He frees himself, strangles Abby (who will later be resuscitated, of course, in Hollywood-ending style), and escapes from the hospital, cutting off his own legs to free himself from his shackles. After a long, legless crawl through sewers, George winds up dead in a crack house and is taken to the morgue. But there, a small miracle occurs: a "mysterious house fly crawls out from George's hair," an escape hatch opens in the middle of George's lifeless brow, and a miniature version of George crawls out and mounts the fly, which takes off like "a little Pegasus" to fly back to Abby. George becomes Abby's invisible companion, riding on his shoulder like a familiar spirit or incubus. The screenplay ends with Abby delivering a eulogy at George's graveside, as the fly takes off with the miniature George "riding like a cowboy . . . directly into an electric bug zapper," where they are "fried instantly."

I read now about Abby and his evil alter ego, George, and I peer cautiously at Gabe's delusions of grandeur and the actuality of his suffering—which, in a sense, fought each other to a draw. It is as if Gabe turned the psychoanalytic dialogue into a debate about cinema, rendered *as* cinema—or at least as screenplay. The talking cure becomes the screenwriter's dilemma, providing illusions for the masses, or unwelcome and unmarketable glimpses of the realities that lead the screen-writer into the grave. Gabe and I once discussed the idea of an entire seminar on "back lot" films (the Coen brothers' *Barton Fink* and Billy Wilder's *Sunset Boulevard* were among our favorites). *The Politics of Dreams*, which incorporates all the genres of cinema, is itself meta-cinema.

When Gabe would visit Carmen in Los Angeles, he would mingle with her circle of friends, including actors, directors, technical people, and, of course, screenwriters. Carmen was writing and acting in plays herself, while holding down a day job at the Writers Guild. As in the academic world, where everyone has his or her book project, in Hollywood, nearly everyone has a script tucked under their arm. The conversation inevitably turns to the question of how one can "take a meeting" with an insider who will open the door to a contract and the ensuing fame and fortune. It is a political field of dreams in which delusions of grandeur are almost completely normal. Carmen noted that Gabe's fantasies fit right into the collective psychosis of aspiring workers in the dream industry.

Gabriel's last words to me on the phone the day of his death were an accusation: "You have never read my screenplays." Of course, I instantly denied this, but there was a terrible, haunting truth to the charge. I think I was incapable of reading his scripts the way I do now, now that they are posthumous records of his struggle. *Then* I was reading them as a father and caregiver in relation to the ongoing life of my son. *Now* I read them in a way that I find much more difficult to classify. Is it an act of mourning, of penance for failing to give him the reading he needed when he was alive? Or am I now free to "do a reading" of the sort that I do as a scholar, linking them to other cases of visionary testimony offered by gifted schizophrenics? Am I reading them to understand him, or his illness? Or in search of something well beyond illness?

When Gabe showed me *The Politics of Dreams*, I was, of course, disturbed by the terrifying figure of George and annoyed by the grandiose projection of Abby the Great, both expressing aspects of Gabe's self-image—or perhaps a caricature of his successful father. I suppose I gave the screenplay a merely symptomatic reading, which in a way is not to read at all but to know beforehand what a text means, to search it for confirmation of a diagnosis—what Kenneth Koch used to call "being the dermatologist at the birthday party," when he admonished us against reading poems this way. I think we all fight this impulse as readers. Most perplexing is the fact that reading someone's writing or listening to them speak "as symptomatic" can be deeply disrespectful, like the incompetent psychoanalyst who tells a patient, "That is just your psychotic grandiosity talking." The worst thing one can say to someone having a psychotic break is "You are having a psychotic break." Of course, since it may also be the only true thing that it is possible to say, silence, lying, and evasion are what one usually resorts to. Beyond that, a symptomatic reading strikes me as too quick to impose closure and apply labels; for example, this is (nothing but) a symptom of schizophrenia. Where is the line between symptom and sympathy? I didn't know then, and I don't know now.

And of course there were questions about the viability of Gabe's scripts as steps toward a career as a screenwriter. I cringe to recall how evasive I had to be when he insisted that I endorse and transmit his scripts to my old friend Henry Louis "Skip" Gates Jr. (Skip is known to the world as the Harvard professor who directs the television series *Finding Your Roots*, but he also appears as a prominent character in Gabe's script for *The Politics of Dreams*, playing Abby's best friend and director.) Skip wrote Gabe an encouraging letter, which he cherished. But Gabe became obsessed with the idea that Skip and I could get Spike Lee to "take a meeting" that would lead to fame and fortune. Anyone who has spent time in Hollywood knows that the idea of "taking a meeting" with an influential player is the Holy Grail of "the industry." Skip tried to let Gabe down easy by telling him, "Gabe, even I can't get Spike to return my calls." He urged Gabe to continue his education in filmmaking and prepare himself to be ready when his moment would come.

I did not get off so easily. I had met Lee briefly in the fall of 2000, when we were on a panel together to discuss the recent release of his film *Bamboozled*. So of course Gabe expected me to call the great director and arrange a meeting. Why wasn't I doing it? Why was I blocking his career when, as his father, I should have been helping him achieve his hopes and dreams?

Nevertheless, Gabe and I could share our love for Lee's film, and we watched *Bamboozled* together many times. He immediately added it to his list of films about screenwriters—in this case, a film about a *television* writer who produces the script for a "New Millennium Minstrel Show" that violates every racial taboo known to American culture. Is the screenwriter, Pierre Delacroix, a victim of the "idiot box" that corrupts his talent? Is he a yuppie sellout, an "Oreo" (black on the outside, white on the inside) who will do anything to preserve his cushy lifestyle and his daily Pilates classes? Or is he going insane, his immersion in the racist stereotypes of "Sambo Art" turning into a psychosis that makes the mechanical dolls of Aunt Jemima and Stepin Fetchit come alive? Gabe lived *inside* this film and took me there with him. And he brought Spike and Skip into supporting roles in his own fantasy world of a brilliant Hollywood career.

Now I try to read his scripts differently, in a way that can only happen when the text is the testimony of someone who has crossed the threshold into madness and death, and left a compelling story about it, along with an unfinished project of understanding. I can no longer bear the symptomatic readings, which confidently label these writings as expressions of this or that syndrome. Who gives a damn whether they are the results of a bipolar disorder or schizophrenia? Like Elyn Saks, Aby Warburg, and William Blake, Gabe lived on the border of a world that most of us know only fleetingly—a world of suffering and shattering both relieved and exacerbated by grandiose fantasies, expressed by a fierce determination to put those fantasies to work and build a world out of the ruins. He was a mental traveler.

CHAPTER TEN

Gabe's Back Pages

The most intimate, directly autobiographical screenplay that Gabe wrote was entitled *My Back Pages*, echoing the title of the visionary 1964 Bob Dylan song with its unforgettable refrain: "But I was so much older then / I'm younger than that now."

Gabe's extensive library was stuffed with books about and CDs of the great troubadour, who according to legend had resided for a time in Chicago's Lawson YMCA. Gabe knew Dylan's lyrics by heart and sang them along with me from his earliest childhood. Gabe spent a lot of time pondering this beautiful but enigmatic line which seemed to reverse time and aging itself. Is Dylan expressing disillusionment with the personal and political idealism of the early folk revival movement for which he was so central? If it was disillusionment, it is very peculiar to describe it as a movement from age to youth. Is he talking about regression? A rebirth? If it were a "sadder but wiser" narrative, one would expect age and maturity to come second. As the poem unfolds, however, the real arc of the narrative is from a former stage of crazy certainty, arrogance, pride, and madness into a present that is left indeterminate, except that in it he is "younger than that now." Consider the first verse and refrain:

Crimson flames tied through my ears
Rollin' high and mighty traps
Pounced with fire on flaming roads
Using ideas as my maps
"We'll meet on edges, soon," said I
Proud 'neath heated brow
Ah, but I was so much older then
I'm younger than that now

Could there be a more precise poetic presentation of schizophrenic thinking? First, the sense of a bonfire in the brain, linked to a grandiose, high-and-mighty entrapment. Isn't schizophrenia exactly this paradoxical feeling of being both sovereign and trapped simultaneously? Those same flames then pounce like a tiger that replicates itself in the conspicuously redundant "fire" and "flaming," all the while depending on "ideas" to keep itself on course. What sort of edgy, marginal "edges" will serve as a rendezvous point Dylan leaves unstated. All he tells us is that this confident speaker is not so sure, so heated, or so proud as he used to be. He has passed through the "fire in the brain" that made him so proud and grandiose. He is humbled now, but paradoxically, against all common sense, "younger." He has moved from fixed ideas and self-styled "wisdom" through madness and suffering to a younger kind of innocence and wonder. Gabe knew very well Blake's famous lines inscribed in a friend's autograph album: "William Blake born 28 Nov' 1757 in London and has died many times since."

Blake's *Songs of Innocence and of Experience* (which I read to Gabe and Carmen when they were children) describes human development as beginning in naivete ("Little Lamb who made thee") and moving on to experience, an encounter with the terror and uncertainty of Blake's Tyger "burning bright, / In the forests of the night," and then on to a third state of higher innocence and prophetic utterance: "Children of the future age, / Reading this indignant page, / Know that in a former time / Love, sweet love, was thought a crime." Gabe's own master narrative of his life followed the pattern laid down in Blake's epic poem *Jerusalem*: "Of the sleep of Ulro! and of the passage through / Eternal Death! and the waking to Eternal Life." The ancient bard of Blake's visionary poetry is in fact "much younger" than the gray-bearded and demented rationalist entrenched among his books in *The Book of Urizen*.

My Back Pages (Gabe's script, that is) tells a story of violence and persecution, punctuated by savage beatings, head injuries, and an attempt by a treacherous girlfriend to inject strychnine into his eye. The script takes us into that dark region that we all saw from outside as a delusion. We never witnessed anything like the conspicuous bodily injuries that Gabe narrates in this film, but they were there, for him. We learned not to argue with him about the reality of what can only be called his "screen memories." His self-diagnosis of PTSD could be merged with a dark narrative of homelessness, addiction, gangs, and high-flying professional-level skateboarding. He was so much older then, having suffered so much, having come to terms with the real world that his parents will never know. In *My Back Pages*, he looked back, inspired by Dylan, from a youthful, rejuvenated perspective, "younger than that now."

And so the look into his back pages is not uniformly dismal. He represents his first beating by a neighbor boy as an outrage and injustice that provokes his father into a confrontation with the boy and his family. This was based in a real memory, provoked by our wonderful friends and neighbors who responded to Gabe's report that their son had beaten him up, not with stern outrage but with noncommittal psychobabble ("What were you feeling when you hit Gabe? Had he done something to make you mad?"). I lost my cool and warned the boy that he had better never do anything like that again, no matter what he was "feeling." I'm sure Janice was embarrassed for me, but Gabe idealized me, at least in this movie, as his father-protector. And he idealized his own past as a visionary homeboy rapper skateboarder nonconformist antihero, running with the wild boys of the racially mixed South Side. In the screenplay, Gabe flaunts his insolence in insulting cops who stop their skateboarding in front of the university library ("Don't you have an appointment at Dunkin' Donuts?"). He is an astronautical sex machine, crying out, "That's one small step for Mankind!" after every orgasm. He goes to college at NYU, gets into philosophy, but finds he already has it all figured out (after all, he was much older then). He takes up drugs and returns to William Blake. He writes a screenplay that disappears from his computer screen every time he tries to print it. And all the while he is accompanied by a muse/guardian angel, named after his sister, Carmen. This muse is a spirit who is always there on his shoulder, chiding him and sharing in whatever he is feeling. She suffers more from the Haldol than Gabe does. Her only wish is a version of the Pinocchio story, to become a real woman.

FIGURE 8. Gabriel Mitchell, "Angelic Muse on shoulder" (n.d.). From *Desolation Row Revisited.*

If *Politics of Dreams* was built around the murderous dialogue of Abby and George, Gabe's alter egos, *My Back Pages* emphasizes the divided images of the women in his life: on the one hand, there is his faithful, vulnerable muse; on the other are the *femmes fatales* who tempt him into meaningless sex and toxic drugs. It is little wonder that a central film in his dreamlife was *Vanilla Sky*, in which the faces of Cameron Diaz (Tom Cruise's "fuck buddy") and Penelope Cruz (his one true love) tend to merge with each other like the Duck-Rabbit in his dream/nightmare life, sleeping for centuries in a cryogenic incubator. Later, in *Crazy Talk*, Cameron Diaz will reappear as "the blonde blue-eyed God I pray to." Is it Diaz or Cruz who finally gave the hero of *Vanilla Sky* the courage to wake up from his dreamlife into the Real by leaping from the roof of a skyscraper?

CHAPTER ELEVEN

Philmworx

If Judge Schreber, perhaps the most famous "person with schizophrenia" in the history of the illness, had the *Memoirs of My Nervous Illness* to make his experiences public, Gabe Mitchell had his website, Philmworx.com. Schreber wrote in the era when neuroscience, forensic psychiatry, and the invention of electricity were transforming the world. Gabe's struggle with schizophrenia corresponded with the age of the computer, the rise of the internet, the dot.com bubble, and social media. Schreber's memoir was printed by a publisher of occult and esoteric writing; Gabe was able to self-publish, thanks to the emergence of the website as a medium of personal expression. Schreber was advised not to publish his memoir, and his psychiatrist actively tried to prevent it. Gabe quite self-consciously portrayed himself as an artist in search of publicity, armed with a medium that breaks down the boundary between private and public life. Gabe underscored his status as an unknown "outsider artist" in tones that alternate between self-deprecation and ironic self-promotion. He brags about his "super power": "the ability to communicate with boring people" and portrays himself as a comic book anti-hero with the astounding ability to consume large quantities of cigarettes and coffee. His dismissal from NYU becomes evidence of his "mutant ability" to transcend the norms of a prestigious university.

In contrast to Schreber, Gabe's autobiographical website does not frame his story as one of illness, mental or otherwise. He portrays himself as the defiant outsider with links to a wide range of accomplishments and a firsthand knowledge of deep suffering—the "real world" of addiction that he often accused his clueless parents (quite accurately) of knowing nothing about. His "junkie" portrait became his business card. His list of film and video credits is a sendup of the inflated CV, including his starring roles as a precocious child actor in Mitchell family home movies. *First Steps* (1974) reveals his gifts at stunts (mainly falling) and slapstick. The three-minute action spectacular, *Third B-Day* (1975) comes complete with a water fight, pie throwing, and clusters of presents being elevated just out of his reach by Grandpa Rocco. Gabe felt that he was a film hero in our own private Ohio, where he spent the first four years of his life. When we moved to Chicago, his private world expanded to include many of the famous writers, artists, and intellectuals who passed through our home. Ursula LeGuin, Jacques Derrida, Edward Said, Henry Louis Gates, Fredric Jameson, Julia Kristeva, Slavoj Žižek, Michael Fried, Robert Morris, Tania Bruguera, Antony Gormley, and many others became part of his fantasy life and his film scripts.

Gabe's website warning to viewers that they "will need a

strong stomach . . . as the artist does a strip tease with his own life-story" echoes the William Burroughs poem "Word," which Gabe had seen his mother perform at Chicago's Green Mill jazz club. In 2007, he made and posted on his website his film *Desolation Row Revisited*, a music video cum flash-card graphic documentary about his life in Humboldt Park among the drug dealers and prostitutes. Gabe, accompanied by Jeff Kust on guitar, provides his own vocals for his rewritten version of Bob Dylan's "Desolation Row." Illustrated with hand-drawn and -lettered scenes that are revealed with each verse, *Desolation Row Revisited* tracks the surreal adventures of an angel-headed hipster/skateboarder, his dog, and a female muse who sits on his shoulder. Oedipus Rex incites a mob (including Michael Jordan making a slam dunk and a flaming cross–waving KKK member) while smashing his car into a fire hydrant. An image of Gabe raising a candle at the grave of Socrates is verbalized as "advertising accidents with a visionary glow." A hooker on a leash is taking money from her handler. She appears shortly thereafter riding in a wheelchair, whipping a harnessed team of her own children, who "already have AIDS," while "on her twenty-second birthday she already is an old maid."

In the film, Gabe places himself between two figures that haunted him in the period after September 11, 2001: the crucified Christ and the Hooded Man of Abu Ghraib. I shared Gabe's obsession with these figures and was, in fact, writing a book about them at the time. Gabe scoured internet databases for Abu Ghraib images, bringing me back political cartoons, sculpture, dolls, photographs, and posters, as well as the complete archive of abuse photos. He helped me understand the iconic character of the Hooded Man of Abu Ghraib as it went viral throughout the world. Gabe's care for me in-

FIGURE 9. Gabriel Mitchell, "Oedipus Rex mob scene" (n.d.). From *Desolation Row Revisited.*

FIGURE 10. Gabriel Mitchell, "Wheelchair 'old maid'" (n.d.). From *Desolation Row Revisited.*

FIGURE 11. Gabriel Mitchell, "Gabe between crucified Jesus and Hooded Man of Abu Ghraib" (n.d.). From *Desolation Row Revisited.*

cluded riding the waves of my passions often with more drive and vision than I did. He uncovered activist art collectives like FreewayBlogger.com and Forkscrew Graphics, who were turning this paradoxical Christ figure into a global symbol of the antiwar movement and an exposé of the Bush-era torture regime. It did not surprise me, then, that Gabe linked Jesus and the Abu Ghraib man in his 2010–11 film, *Crazy Talk.* He juxtaposed the iconic torture victims with American psychiatry's collaboration in developing the CIA's "enhanced interrogation techniques," a systematic and specific form of "madness production," or, more to the point, technology for driving people insane, right alongside the patent madness of the War on Terror. We absorbed repeated viewings of the classic film *The Manchurian Candidate,* with its treatment of brainwashing and American paranoia.

As I watched Gabe's art unfold in the last five years of his life, his most creative period, I could see him struggling to work through and appropriate all sorts of influences. Occasionally I would see my own work being recycled along with Janice's music and Carmen's ideas and her presence as the guardian angel/muse. But Gabe was rapidly absorbing numerous other influences as well. He was immersed in weekly classes with a Who's Who of Chicago film critics, including Michael Wilmington, Roger Ebert, and Jonathan Rosenbaum, and he and I joined the Godard Group at the University of Chicago, whose members included the film scholars Miriam Hansen, Tom Gunning, and Yuri Tsivian. The group worked through the intricate montage of Godard's *Histoire du cinéma* in nine weeks. Every Tuesday evening, we would watch one hour of Godard's epic *twice*, gobbling up pizza in the short break between the two screenings. The second time through, we would pause the film frequently for discussion of stills, shots, and scenes, wallowing in the encyclopedic knowledge of film history commanded by Gunning, Hansen, and Tsivian and occasionally dipping into the numerous references to the history of painting (Turner and Goya, Bosch and El Greco) or the clips of newsreel footage from the disastrous twentieth century. After taking intensive night courses through the University of Chicago's continuing education program, including courses on Hitchcock, Almodóvar, Buñuel, the Coen brothers, Ingmar Bergman, and John Ford alongside seminars on the silent film era and the subsequent Hollywood Code years, Gabe too was becoming a walking encyclopedia of film history. In 2010–11, he began to synthesize cinema with the graphic novel, particularly the genre of the schlemiel as superhero— Spider-Man, as well as his self-portrait as the caped G-Unit— and the fatal feminine mystique of the world-destroying Dark

FIGURE 12. Gabriel Mitchell, "G-Unit superhero" (n.d.).

THE THUGISH BICYCLE RIDER IS MISSING BOTH WHEEL AND LEG

FIGURE 13. Gabriel Mitchell, "One-legged cyclist" (n.d.). From *Desolation Row Revisited.*

Phoenix, who bears a startling resemblance to the winged muse on his shoulder.

He inspired the Superhero Film Society (mentioned earlier), consisting of graphic novel scholar Hillary Chute, media and game theorist Patrick Jagoda, and myself, regaling us with backstories from the world of Marvel Comics, which had broken with the old DC-Superman model to explore "damaged" superheroes—like himself. The time was rapidly passing when I thought of myself as an influence on Gabe; the tables were turning, and I felt increasingly swept up in his artistic ambitions and his ever-expanding archive of films, music, and books. I frankly could not keep up when he turned to Ray Kurzweil's concept of "the singularity" and explained to me that *The Singularity Is Near* was written with him in mind.

Kurzweil's singularity fit perfectly with Gabe's conviction

that a radical transformation in human consciousness was coming in the near future. Kurzweil predicted that by 2045 artificial intelligence would outstrip human, turning human beings into a new species of cyborgs able to transcend their physical and mental limitations. Gabe's universe was riding the utopian wave of techno-optimism that linked the 1960s counterculture to the emergent cyberculture, the *Whole Earth Catalog* to *Wired* magazine, my generation to his. Marshall McLuhan's prophecies of an electronically extended nervous system seemed to be on the verge of fulfillment and allowed Gabe to see his schizophrenia as a symptom of the new, emergent consciousness, beyond capitalism and the collective self-destructiveness of the human species.

These technological issues help to explain why, at the same time that Gabe was exploring the dark confusion of individual and collective madness, he was also turning to what looked like the opposite extreme: the world of science, mathematics, and hyperrationality. In 2011 Gabe completed a new film, *Grid Theory*, exploring the history of visionary geometry and cosmology. Sketched out on the drafting table in his apartment, which looked out over the modernist monuments of downtown Chicago, and with a marimba soundtrack provided by Janice, *Grid Theory* traces the evolution of diagrams from their function as magical talismans to models of the structure of life itself, the fourfold double helix of DNA. He began to elaborate these geometrical conceptions in the form of a sculptural object he called the *Infinite Cube*, for which he made models out of wire and tape.

The final realization of this vision is now in the University of Chicago's Smart Museum of Art. A three-foot mirrored-glass cube containing a wire matrix of one thousand omnidirectional LED lights, Antony Gormley's *Infinite Cube* opens up

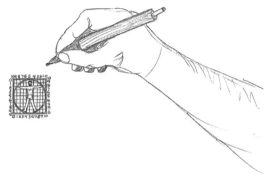

EDUCATION PASS THE
TEST
THE MIND NEEDS SEEDS TO
SOW

FIGURE 14. Gabriel Mitchell, "Hand drawing grid" (n.d.). From *Desolation Row Revisited.*

endless vistas that shift and shimmer as the beholder moves around it, producing a sense of rigorous mathematical order and vertigo at the same time. Gabe had met Gormley on a visit to London, and again when the artist visited Chicago as the guest of the annual Humanities Festival. The two of them had an instant rapport and went off tramping along the lakefront on a frigid November evening, looking for possible sites for Gormley's work. Gabe gave Antony one of his model cubes, and after his death, Antony called us up. "I would like to make Gabe's cube," he said, "if that's all right with you." Needless to say, it was more than all right. The work is based in Gabe's need for a sense of order in his own disorderly mental life, and yet it also insists on the experience of infinity, alluding to Blake's theory of the Vortex as the figure that locates the infinite in the finite.

FIGURE 15. Gabriel Mitchell, "Diagram of DNA" (n.d.).

Gabe pillaged the images from Hannah Higgins's *The Grid Book* to make *Grid Theory*, a cinematic history of the diagrammatic and geometric imagination from the ancient world to modern architecture and beyond. Alongside his film, *Philosomentary*, an idiosyncratic history of philosophy from Socrates to the moderns, and *A Brief History of Light*, from Plato's Cave to cinema, *Grid Theory* was Gabe's attempt to put it all

FIGURE 16. Antony Gormley, *Infinite Cube* (2014). © the artist. Mirrored glass with internal copper wire matrix of 1,000 hand-soldered omnidirectional LED lights, 91.4 × 91.4 × 91.4 cm. Collaboration between Antony Gormley and Gabriel Mitchell. Smart Museum of Art, The University of Chicago.

together. "The Grid," he declared in a talk he gave to a University of Chicago seminar in 2011, is "what kept me alive" through the dark times of psychosis and addiction. It was also an attempt to "square the circle" by inventing a new set of anti-Cartesian geometrical principles. Gabe's grid, in contrast

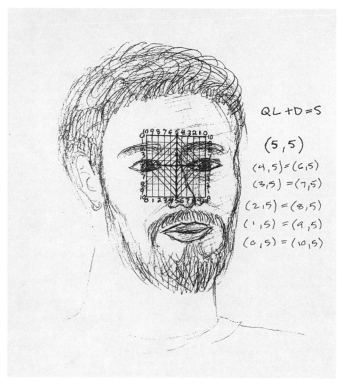

The equations visible in the figure:

$$QL + D = S$$

$$(5,5)$$

$$(4,5) = (6,5)$$
$$(3,5) = (7,5)$$
$$(2,5) = (8,5)$$
$$(1,5) = (9,5)$$
$$(0,5) = (10,5)$$

FIGURE 17. Gabriel Mitchell, "Self-portrait with grid" (n.d.).

to Cartesian coordinates, had no place for negative numbers, and instead of starting from a central axis of zero, it worked as a procession of positive integers around the perimeter.

I saw Gabe's grid theory as, at best, a poetic metaphor, at worst, a symptom of grandiosity. I was troubled by his vehement insistence that the grid was not just his psychological safety net but a metaphysical truth about the universe that mathematicians would ultimately come to appreciate. He wrote to scientist Norman MacLeod about his theory, and his related ambition to defy the mathematicians and succeed in squaring the circle. Norman replied with a masterful explanation of why mathematicians had abandoned this question but also why he thought Gabe's proposed method for solving it made perfect sense. Why did I insist on distinguishing between a poetic mathematics and a "real" mathematics? Gabe was not just an outsider artist, but an outsider filmmaker and an outsider mathematician. It seems crucial to these roles that they involve steadfast defiance of fatherly spokesmen for the reality principle.

Gabe ignored copyright restrictions and stole freely from media sources, taking Bob Dylan's tune and setting his own lyrics to it or appropriating clips from Hollywood films without permission. We wasted a lot of breath warning him that he would encounter great difficulties if he tried to put his mash-ups of stolen footage into public circulation. His answer was perfectly reasonable: "Godard gets away with it. Why not me?" I once asked him straight out: "Look. Do you want honest, constructive criticism from me, or do you want me to tell you that everything is just fine?" He did not hesitate: "I don't need your so-called constructive criticism. Just tell me that it's great and we will be fine." I had a conversation with Bill Ayers about this. Bill was often Gabe's film buddy when I was unavailable, a magnanimous comrade whose most negative pronouncement on a movie is "it's watchable." Bill's advice was clear and wise: "Let the world take care of sending messages about reality; the parental unit is very badly qualified for this role, since it takes the caregiving situation back to early childhood and induces forms of regression on all sides. Your job is not to be his critic, much less his censor, but to do what you are doing best—staying his friend and supporter as much as possible." Gabe's last film, created a few months before his death, was about Bill.

The version of Philosomentary on Gabe's website is a per-

LEAVING BEHIND ALL THE GHOSTS UPON DESOLATION ROW

FIGURE 18. Gabriel Mitchell, "Drunken Muse with bottle" (n.d.). From *Desolation Row Revisited.*

versely weird "preview." Carmen is wearing whiteface and reading a film script, a fairy tale about a young man's tragic experience of unrequited love. Her listener is Gabe, immersed in the fabulous narrative he is hearing: a children's story with a moral ("forgiveness is divine") at the end. The whole scene feels somehow "symptomatic"—embarrassingly regressive and infantile—but visually it is even more disturbing in its parodic restaging of the psychoanalytic dialogue. Gabe lies on the couch facing away from the storyteller, hearing his own story read back to him by his own muse/sister. The roles of speaker and listener, sitting and reclining, have been reversed, as if the doctor were put in the position of storyteller, not interpreter, reading and reciting the "once upon a time" narrative of the patient. The psychoanalytic dialogue has been transformed into a kind of solipsistic Gothic monologue, or self-ventriloquism, as if Gabe were bringing to life the numerous cartoons in which he shows himself with a muse/fairy hovering over his shoulder, reciting his story, and suffering along with him.

Perhaps this is Gabe's own screen memory of his broken heart, and his long process of healing. R. D. Laing tells us that schizophrenia may be nothing more than a broken heart—not just a dividing of the self into polarities of thought and feeling, but a shattering of the self. That is why the person with schizophrenia often feels beset on all sides by enemies and energies, or, even worse, friends and loved ones who are betraying him. Even the physical environment can feel hostile, to the extent that the body cannot tolerate cold sensation (notice the number of homeless people wearing down jackets on a summer day). When Gabe was a boy, we often had trouble convincing him that it was time to shed his winter coat.

Aside from *Desolation Row Revisited* and *Crazy Talk*, Gabe's website betrays very little of the dark, paranoid, and suffering side of his condition. His final work for it, composed in the months just before his death, was *Bill Ayers: Thoughts & Memories*, a montage of antiwar protest images with a voiceover of Bill reading from his memoir, *Fugitive Days*, about his travails on the borders between madness and sanity in 1968. In *Crazy Talk*, Gabe interviewed Bill about a photograph of him as a crazy 1960s revolutionary, comparing it to images of the Tea Party political movements of 2009–10—movements that have now achieved real political power. An essential part of Gabe's emergence from the dark night of schizophrenia was this recognition that he was not alone in exploring the frontiers of madness and sanity, that he had company in the lives of revolutionaries, prophets, martyrs, artists, and visionaries, not to mention the anonymous outsiders, the homeless, abandoned, or imprisoned who suffer madness, more or less quietly. Could he make a film from their stories, their myths?

CHAPTER TWELVE

The Immoral Career
of the Caregiver

What about the little world of the nuclear family? The role
of caregivers in cases of mental illness is generally neglected
in favor of attention to the person suffering. The family and
friends of the ill person are usually treated as assistants or ad-
juncts to the real work that must be done by the "patient" (he
must "really want to change") and the doctor. The doctor is
often forbidden by law even to talk with the caregiving team
in any detail about the patient's condition. At worst, families
are regarded as the cause of the patient's condition; at best,
as hopelessly incompetent, having given up their responsibility for the patient and turned him over to institutions and
professionals.

This support team often finds itself in impossible situations. Suppose, for instance, that the family is scattered, and
all the responsibility devolves on one or two people. Almost

inevitably, there is little consensus about causes, cures, and diagnoses. Had we caused Gabe's condition with our lax parenting or our use of recreational drugs? Should we be addressing his condition as schizophrenia, manic depression, or a schizotypal personality disorder? Is the medical model itself fatally deficient? R. D. Laing's analysis of schizophrenia largely depended on a picture of a dysfunctional nuclear family with an absent father and an unloving mother, and so his therapeutic answer often demanded a separation from the family, sometimes the adoption of a new family, and even a process of "re-birthing." At the other extreme is the warehousing of the mentally ill and their subjection to involuntary confinement and medication. Elyn Saks's autobiography of her struggle with schizophrenia emphasizes the horrors of imposed restraints (from padded cells to straitjackets) in American mental hospitals, even as she concedes that her own survival depended crucially on finding effective medications and talk therapy.

When a person is falling into a mental illness, there is often a double trauma. First, there are the symptoms themselves (depression, anxiety, paranoia, anger, delusions, and hallucinations). The diagnosis then arrives as a secondary trauma that may be experienced by the patient as even worse than the primary symptoms. It may, of course, be some comfort to have a professional person assign a name to one's suffering. But unlike the diagnosis of a physical illness, and the decision about treatment, the diagnosis of mental illness is not just filled with uncertainty; it produces at the same time a terrible certainty, a fatal stigma that can be deeply damaging to the person's prospects for relationships and employment and, of course, to their self-image.

Schizophrenia in particular is often regarded as a kind of

death sentence; like the word "cancer," it produces a shudder. This is not only a matter of the high frequency of suicide among those suffering from schizophrenia but also the feeling on the part of the patient that they are undergoing a kind of social death, being "cast out." And the casting out is, of course, being perpetrated by those closest to the patients—their immediate family. As Erving Goffman notes in his classic essay "The Moral Career of the Mental Patient," this first or "pre-patient" phase of the process "typically begins with the experience of abandonment, disloyalty, and embitterment." The person has become difficult to live with, is unable to work and function as a member of society or the family in a normal way, and a mental hospital seems like the only answer. This course of action varies widely with the economic status of the family and the patient. The Kennedy family was able to conceal the illness of Jack Kennedy's sister for many years, and wealthy individuals can afford private asylums where the treatment and conditions are much nicer than the typical public facility.

It is almost inevitable, then, that the onset of a mental illness in an individual will produce a crisis in the group of people closest to them. Often perceived as traitors by their afflicted loved one, they are likely to suffer feelings of guilt, confusion, anger, and resentment. They will look for someone to blame—themselves; illegal drugs and bad companions; incompetent doctors; a toxic social environment; or each other. People do not go crazy alone; they take their families with them into the land of mental illness. Wealthy families usually contrive, as the Kennedys did, to conceal the existence of the mentally ill relative. Sometimes they are treated as "special" and allowed to go through life without working; with enough family resources, an alternative career as an artist may be manageable, and the arts often serve as a kind of asylum in this sense. In the worst case, their families abandon them and try to forget about their existence. In some extreme cases, the caregivers may find themselves in danger from the mental patient and only able to provide support at arm's length through intermediaries. At a NAMI meeting, Janice met a woman who had to change her address and phone number to keep her son from finding her and killing her. She used intermediaries to keep him housed and provided with the basic necessities of life.

Gabriel's schizophrenia seemed to be at the center of contrary forces in our family life, but it actually brought us closer together. Janice and I had to hold daily conferences about the management of Gabe's life, from finances to keeping appointments and taking medications to long-term questions, such as when we could be away and where he should be living. It had become clear that Gabe's living at home was impossible for us and bad for him. He needed to live apart from us, even at the cost of his conviction that we were "throwing him out." At a more micro level, we had to find ways to cope with the stress of dealing with his rapid mood changes, the "triggers" that would send him into a rage or depression, or his uncontrollable flights of fantasy. We had to walk a tightrope between encouraging his dreams and ambitions on the one hand and providing a reality test on the other. Generally, our strategy was one of humoring him, letting him tell elaborate stories, including his lurid screen memories of how he came to be ill. His self-diagnosis as a victim of trauma rather than schizophrenia was couched in a detailed account of being beaten with a tire iron in a face-off with gang members. This inevitably became a collective memory, one of those family stories that gets repeated until it becomes a bedrock fact.

In a film that Carmen is making about Gabe's life, she will include an investigation into the facts of the matter with the close friends who (in Gabe's telling) administered the beating as part of some esoteric gang initiation. We learned not to challenge these stories, even though it was alarming to see him completely locked into memories that bore little relation to reality as we knew it.

Gabe's schizophrenia also brought us together by giving us a common enemy. I hated schizophrenia for what it was doing to my son. I sometimes regarded it as a demon that needed to be exorcised, and indeed, it did sometimes feel like a form of possession by an alien spirit. It helped, of course, that Gabe was fighting it as well. But the target of the fight was elusive and shifty: Was it the symptoms? The conditions that aggravated the symptoms? The ineffectual doctors and institutions? The medications that quieted the voices but also muffled all the thoughts he wanted to have? Like Judge Schreber, Gabe would never give in but was adamant and passionate in his delusions, and this put a strain on all of us. The subjective reality of his visions and their attendant beliefs could not be doubted. Gabe was verbally adept and firmly convinced of his own powers of reason. He was always thrusting his arm through imaginary windows, asserting his grip on realities that we could not see.

For example, we had to hold our tongues when he indulged in fantasies about his supposed girlfriend, Cricket, the young woman he obsessed over at NYU. When Carmen interviewed Cricket after Gabe's death, it only deepened the mystery. Cricket told Carmen that she was almost completely unaware of how serious his delusions about her were. She also said that she "adored him" for his sweetness and creativity. But "adoration" in Gabe's mind could only be taken literally to mean that she was destined to be his life partner. We met with her (and with her mother) a number of times, both before and after the onset of Gabe's illness, and always found the same obliviousness to the outsize role she was playing in his fantasy life. Whatever the reality behind Gabe's delusions, for us it was always a sure sign of impending trouble when Cricket's name began to crop up in his conversation.

Living with a gifted person with schizophrenia, especially one as verbally eloquent as Gabriel, can be a real trial. We had numerous "kitchen debates," in which he assured us that there was nothing wrong with him and the problem was with us. He routinely indicted our comfortable, bourgeois lifestyle, out of touch with the real world of the streets. He also had an uncanny ability to turn the tables on us and trigger our own anxieties with accusations about the emptiness of our twenty-five-year marriage (now in its fiftieth), the hollow, pointlessness of our lives, or the futility of our misguided efforts to help him.

Gabe's schizophrenia had the effect of filling our supposedly hollow marriage with an abundance of things to talk about. We were always comparing notes about potentially common reality principles in the midst of delusion and misery. It turns out that my own form of misery loves a limited company; it contracted my circle of close friends at the same time my academic network was growing. I withdrew from engagement with the University of Chicago and retreated into teaching, research, and writing. I could feel Gabe becoming my best friend, which carried a dark anxiety along with it: What if he were to become my *only* friend? Would I have to cross over completely into his delusional world? Why not? Why not quit my job and make movies with him? I seriously considered this, even talking about it with a very few people.

In truth, I was scared of taking that step. I chickened out. Another could have, should have, would have. But when I think soberly about it now, I suspect it would have been a huge mistake for me to move in on his major ambition.

There is nothing quite like the dynamics of a normal neurotic family with a psychotic son. Since neurosis is all about repression of instincts and fantasy in favor of reality, and psychosis is about repression of reality in favor of fantasy and delusion, their combination can produce a perfect storm of miscommunication and anxiety. At best, it leads to an uneasy standoff in which the neurotic caregivers are so focused on managing realities that they cannot sympathize with the psychotic's fantasy life, stonewalling its expression either with blank silence or (worse) with vehement dismissals. The kind of patient and proactive attentiveness that a skilled therapist could give to these fantasies was almost impossible for us. They certainly gave Janice and me something to talk about over dinner every night. What is he saying today? Did he bring up Cricket? How did he say he was feeling? Are the nightmares worse?

Our chief refuge in this perfect storm was Carmen. Although she was living on the West Coast, she provided a constant third voice in the ongoing struggle between Gabe and us, whom he called his "parental units." Gabe would sometimes exhibit the classic symptoms of flat affect, resistance to being touched, and a hair-trigger temper. But Carmen could get through to him, partly because she was most definitely *not* occupying a parental role, and in fact had a sisterly solidarity with him *against* the parents. He could vent his frustration with us by opening up to her, and she was skilled at steering him back toward taking responsibility for his own life. And on his visits to her in Los Angeles, he was able to mix with her circle of "creative" friends: young actors, directors, and screenwriters, all dreaming of success in Hollywood, just like Gabe. "In Hollywood," Carmen often remarked, "Gabe's grandiosity about a brilliant career in the movies makes him sound just like everyone else." Carmen played a central role in leading Gabe back from the early dark years of his illness into a measure of happiness and creativity. In Gabe's screenplays, she is the benign guardian angel who accompanies him everywhere in "My Back Pages" and who, in his cartoons for *Desolation Row Revisited*, gets drunk with him in the near-comatose world of Haldol. His sister-muse stayed with him through every form of intoxication, both negative and positive.

For us as a caregiving family, then, the mental and emotional condition of our beloved son was a daily burden that settled into an array of roles. Janice was the practical minder and guardian, dealing with questions of insurance, medications, Social Security benefits, and his finances. She was also his mentor as an artist, drawing on her long experience as a composer and performer struggling to make a career, and he was a loyal helper with her concerts and videos, serving as cameraman, stagehand, and usher. Her choral setting of Blake's "Mad Song" (written when Gabe was a baby) frames the soundtrack of his film *Crazy Talk*. He stole the music, of course, without mentioning Janice in the credits. Janice was able to reinforce his sense of his struggle as an artistic one, not just a medical or psychiatric matter. When he complained that no one was taking his films seriously, Janice could play a strong hand with him, welcoming him to the reality of life as an artist. There is nothing like being a composer of avant-garde music to give you a sense of how difficult it is to succeed as a serious artist in this country today. Janice was his artistic reality check.

Carmen was his spiritual adviser, engaging in long talks on the telephone and hosting him for welcome getaways to Los Angeles. I was his film, sports, and books buddy, talking with him on the phone about the exploits of the Chicago Bulls, sharing filmic immersion therapy in the Godard Group and our Superhero Film Society, and reading with him everything from Blake to Nietzsche to Deleuze and Guattari. I am still uncertain whether the chapter on schizoanalysis in *Anti-Oedipus* was a good thing for him to read. But we found solidarity in Gabe's projection of the symptoms of psychosis onto capitalism, racism, colonialism, torture, slavery, confinement, drugs, abuse, alienation, abandonment, war, and genocide. These generalized symptoms of collective madness were a welcome alternative to blaming ourselves, or Gabe's friends, or bad DNA, or the shortcomings of psychiatry. Between Frantz Fanon's critique of the psychopathology of colonialism and America's demented War on Terror, Gabe learned to politicize madness, to see the individual form of it as an imposed identity, a social construction that has deep existential consequences. He was increasingly determined to live his life as a member of a minority defined by disability status, an outsider from the world of normally "abled" people. His emerging militancy about schizophrenia—his insistence on "coming out" to people right away—was not helping him in this respect. I advised him to treat his condition as a private matter, only to be divulged when he knew the person well. Like most of my good advice, it didn't take. He watched his friends grow up, get married, and have kids in the decade after the onset of his illness. "When is my life going to start?" he asked.

CHAPTER THIRTEEN

On the Case of Gabriel Mitchell

What if the answer were right here, right now, with this book? Isn't this precisely "a life," at least in writing, that is, a "biography"? Isn't this the life that Gabe wanted? To be the hero of his own story? Not really. He has clearly become the hero of *my* story. It is not the story I wanted for him or dreamed of as his future. He was already writing his own life in his films.

A dear friend asked me as I began writing Gabe's life story, "Why do you want to turn your son into a case?" "Is that what I am doing?" I asked. The question stopped me cold. Could this be one of those cold cases that provides television detectives with an obsessive mission in life? Early on, I wanted to imagine foul play, a murder most foul. What if he didn't jump but was pushed? After all, I asked, why didn't he leave a note? But then there was the cinematic suicide note provided by *Crazy Talk*'s images of falling and flying, so obvious in retrospect. So what if there were no mystery to be solved, no way to breathe life and warmth into the cold case?

When Janice and I visited the funeral home the day after Gabe's death, we were advised not to view his body because the sight would haunt us forever. We insisted on touching it instead, encased in many layers of white fabric in a cold white room. It seemed essential, somehow, to see the shrouded form, just to take in the familiar proportions and scale of our son's shattered body, to lay our hands on him through the winding sheet. Could I unwind it with writing, the only thing I know how to do? Only if I could accept that I would be turning him into a case and writing a case study. I was comforted in this by Wittgenstein's remark, "the world is all that is the case," but I wanted to turn it inside out and insist that a case is all the world. Not "a" world, but "the" world that dies with the individual who takes it with him. I knew that my life of Gabe would be grounded in, but not bounded by, the singular, specific case of his existence in the world and his departure from it. A case is more than an example; it exceeds the typical or exemplary, and opens onto a world, in fact, onto many worlds.

Practitioners depend on the concept of the case in many fields, from medicine to sociology to criminology and forensics. The "case history" has a special salience in psychoanalysis, since an important aim of the classic talking cure is to encourage the analysand to reveal without self-censorship their private world, which may be a secret even from them. That history is then schematized and labeled with a ready-made stock of stereotypes. You are depressed, bipolar, schizophrenic, demented, hysterical, narcissistic, deluded, neurotic, obsessive. The case history in psychiatry stands in a space between the singularity of a particular person and the generalizations that declare that you have (or are) "a case of" a specific type of mental illness. The psychiatric case involves a normative category involving a judgment about "disorder" or "illness" as opposed to orderly normality and health. This puts it in the paradoxical position of producing a normalized picture of abnormality, in contrast, say, to biology, where the general category of a species is grounded in "good specimens" rather than deviations from the norm and where the paradox of "normal deviations" may be calibrated. As for the legal case, the saying is that "hard cases make bad law": only "easy" ones are clear cut. Mental disorders are, by definition, hard cases, frequently anomalous, always more complex than the stereotype applied to them.

Nothing like the rigorousness of biological taxonomy or case law is possible in the "mental case." This is partly because of the infinite complexity of the human individual as such but also because the boundaries of the individual are themselves often in question in the psychiatric disorder: relations to family, to the social environment, to the individual's history, class, gender, and racial identity all play a role in determining what the individual's case looks like. The basic question of what belongs to or is relevant to the case may be difficult to specify. Like the *Infinite Cube*, a finite box with windows mirroring endless depths, the soul is a universe. The family, the community, and even the larger historical world are all reflected within the case.

This becomes even more complicated when the case history is being written, not by an "objective" psychiatrist who looks up a list of symptoms in the DSM and compares the case with others, but by a family member who is *inside* the case, deeply implicated in it. In the present case of Gabriel Mitchell, his father is writing this case history primarily as a personal memoir interrupted by amateur forays into analysis. A psychoanalyst would no doubt find this father-son dynamic central to whatever structure the case has, as if Oedipus's father had returned from the grave, along with Oedipus's mother, sister, relatives, and friends, to weigh in on his complex. Or as if Judge Schreber's father, whose strict disciplinary regimes were often faulted for Schreber's illness, would return to tell his son's story. So in the case of Gabriel Mitchell, the picture that emerges includes the author of the case history and many others who played a role in his life story. So this story is hopelessly compromised, built on nothing but conflicting interests: an impossible wish to understand in the face of the mystery of Gabe's suicide; a sense of justice, of somehow rectifying the terrible unfairness of his death; a desire to give him the fame he so longed for; a confession of failure to save or protect him; an unending, unreasoning denial of his death; and an increasing acceptance of my own.

Unable to crack the case, or to close it, I find some comfort in Leonard Cohen's lines: "Ring the bells that still can ring / Forget your perfect offering / There is a crack in everything / That's how the light gets in."

I have already referred several times to the canonical case of gifted schizophrenia, Judge Daniel Paul Schreber, the psychotic Chief Justice of the Supreme Court of Saxony, Germany, in the 1880s. A brilliant jurist, Schreber went stark, raving mad and then managed to write his *Memoirs of My Nervous Illness* (1903), complete with a new theology in which Schreber himself was to play the role of redeemer by turning himself into a woman to be impregnated by God, thus breeding a new improved version of the human species.

When Gabe was in a mood to accept that he had—or was—a case of schizophrenia, he identified with the company of artists like William Blake, who tried to "put madness to work" and create world systems out of their imagination. Gabe wanted to defy Foucault's notion that madness is unproductive, incapable of producing an oeuvre. Gabe resolved to make madness the material and the method of his work. His labor, then, was the struggle with schizophrenia itself, a complex resistance to and reflection on its disabling symptoms and stigmas. High-functioning persons with schizophrenia are sometimes able not just to maintain a semblance of normality but also to explore and report on their experiences, transforming them into insights that speak eloquently to us ordinary neurotics. "Perhaps we will learn," wrote R. D. Laing, "to accord to so-called schizophrenics who have come back to us . . . no less respect than the often no less lost explorers of the Renaissance. If the human race survives, future men will, I suspect, look back on our enlightened epoch as a veritable Age of Darkness." Laing was not romanticizing schizophrenia. He knew that most of these lost explorers will never be heard from, only the gifted and lucky few "who have come back to us." And most who come back, like Gabe, do so only partially, providing glimpses of the unknown limits of human consciousness but never achieving "the work" that could make them famous, remembered.

I use the word *gifted* with a full sense of its ambiguity. Thinkers from Marcel Mauss to Jacques Derrida have taught us that the gift is a double-edged sword. Failure to reciprocate the gift, according to Mauss, is an occasion for shame, even slavery. The Greek gods gave the mad prophetess Cassandra the gift of prophecy but accompanied it with the curse of never being believed. Hercules is gifted with irresistible strength, which he uses to cleanse the world of monsters, even to play the role of Atlas and hold the world on his shoulders. But he cannot vanquish the internal monster known as madness, which leads him to murder his entire family. Among the most common accursed gifts of schizophrenia is, aside from a generalized grandiosity, visions of gods and angels.

Schizophrenia sometimes endows its victim with a heightened, excessive mindfulness in which all the normal, controllable functions of the mind/brain (dreams, fantasy, memory, associations, the omnipotence of thoughts) are amplified, exaggerated, and rerouted into eccentric pathways. In Schreber's case, his hyperactive thought processes left him looking vacant and catatonic to observers. That is why schizophrenic withdrawal from the outer into an inner world is so mysterious but also so revealing about what it means to have something called a "mental life" in the first place. Carmen described Gabe during the onset of his illness as transformed from the gregarious, generous person we had known, his chronic dreaminess turned into a hollow, staring catatonia. When Gabe was born, Carmen had regarded him as "a present: a beautiful doll just for me." Something of this and more returned toward the end of his struggle with schizophrenia: "A second incarnation of Gabe emerged. A more courageous one than the one I'd known in childhood, a fighter, but also one who would literally give you the coat off his back." Gabe became a great giver of gifts saturated with thought. His drawings, models, money, clothes, and poems were yours without a second thought. He returned the cursed gift of schizophrenia by holding a mirror up to it, like Perseus confronting Medusa with her own image.

Gabe wanted to connect his journey through madness not just to the famous gifted schizophrenics but also to the unknown "outsiders" like himself—the obscure eccentrics and artists, the discharged veterans with PTSD, the anonymous vagabonds and homeless who roam the streets of major cities and the backroads of rural America, sometimes merging with the floods of refugees and the precarious communities of displaced persons. He told me that the most important lesson in Foucault's *History of Madness* was its attempt to tell the "history of that silence" where insanity reigns. That is why he mocked his own obscurity on the website that he hoped would bring him fame: "First thing you should know about me is that most of my great accomplishments can't fit on a website. If the stuff that I have done is known to you already, then you are a friend or family type person. I wouldn't mind people knowing every last thing I ever did in my life. I have no shame!" As a "family type person," I hear the rhyme implicit in these lines between fame and shame, the simultaneous tones of grandiosity and irony, bragging and self-deprecating comedy.

Along with the grandiosity came a loss of boundaries accompanied by extraordinary selflessness—it is no wonder that his first impulse was to join the homeless and to give away his winter coat. When he started making *Crazy Talk*, street people were among the first he interviewed. In the film, he portrays his encounter with what we used to call a "sandwich man," a homeless man wearing a cardboard sign reading "Girlfriend kidnapped by Ninjas . . . need money for Ransom and Kung-fu Lessons." Without hesitation, Gabe gives the man five bucks and asks if he can interview him. As the police sirens wail in the background, the smiling sandwich man thanks him for his generosity and Gabe scans his sign with his camera. When I would walk the same street with him, however, Gabe would complain that the panhandlers were constantly bothering him because he had become known as a soft touch for money and cigarettes.

Was the grandiosity the condition that made the generosity possible, or vice versa? As Gabe and I began gathering images for his cinematic history of madness, I began to see the contradictory character of the images he wanted to collect, the way they ranged from figures of animality to divinity, nonsense to rationality, suffering to ecstasy, solitary pain to charismatic power. In *Crazy Talk*, Gabe removed the wild sounds of the wind that accompany the images of Tom Cruise's suicidal plunge from a skyscraper in *Vanilla Sky* and replaced them with the calm voice-over of psychologist Ethan Watters describing the way our globalizing culture is "homogenizing the way the world goes mad." It is as if the slow-motion vision of suicide is slowed even further by a quiet reflection on the globalization of psychiatry. Gabe wanted to resist the reductive tendencies of Western medicine, even while accepting it in the form of an antipsychotic called Zyprexa. No borders or distinctions would be allowed to interfere with his ambition to trace the infinite varieties of madness across cultures and historical periods. Everything from the shaman and the crazy clown to the silent mystic, the insane king, and the mad scientist were to serve as material. Gabe saw the "mad masters" of Jean Rouch's documentary about the ritual parodies of British colonialism in West Africa as a gateway into the world of collective insanity as a mode of political resistance. He viewed Spike Lee's film *Bamboozled* as a prophetic fantasy of the mass hysteria that would accompany a successful revival of blackface minstrelsy in a supposedly postracial era. It soon became clear to me that there would be no limits to the atlas of madness I was assembling for his film.

But we had to start somewhere. In the winter of 2011, we put together a seminar entitled "Seeing Madness." I can't recall whose idea it was first. It just seemed to jell as we began to think about what the impossible atlas would contain. The visual archive of Sander Gilman's *Seeing the Insane* was an early stop, followed by a plunge into the bottomless pit of movies about mental patients, psychiatrists, and asylums. But *Crazy Talk* began in darkness and midsentence as the voice of Carmen is heard asking "what mental illness is in reality . . . because I think there are a lot of films that kind of misrepresent it." The aim was clearly not merely to compile a bunch of examples, to make madness visible, but also to see *through* madness as a critical framework and to see beyond it.

If Gabe had lived, we would certainly have been tracking the phenomenon of the mad sovereign leading a deluded collectivity. Donald Trump's presidency would have been central to our archive, since images of his political base, the "Mad Tea Party," were already featured in *Crazy Talk*. From the biblical Nebuchadnezzar to Plato's "Ship of Fools" to King Lear to Descartes's "Evil Genius" to the mad King George III, Gabe was leading me into a labyrinth in which power, madness, and religion were deeply interwoven. As we moved out from the reassuring narratives that tell us that the god and ministers of Christianity are wise and good, and that "Western Civilization" has been a force for rational enlightenment, we discovered that "the gods must be crazy" when seen from the standpoint of an African Bushman, as the 1980 film by that title instructs us. Our seminar's viewing of Ken Russell's *The Devils*, which deals with the deranged pursuit of witches, exorcism, and demon possession in seventeenth-century France, led us into the darkest regions of mass hysteria and state-sponsored violence.

The seminar became a wild ride from the crazy gods and heroes of Classical Greece to the Medieval Fool to the tormented scenes of Hieronymus Bosch, the ecstasies of Saint Teresa, Dürer's *Melancholia*, Goya's and Blake's Mad Men to the liberation of the insane during the French Revolution and the rise of the nineteenth-century asylum with its "tranquilizer chairs," confinement beds, water cures, and electrical shock. We took in Louis Sass's thesis in *Madness and Modernism* that the combination of self-consciousness, alienation, and withdrawal associated with schizophrenia was endemic to the aesthetics of modernism, exemplified by the "paranoid methods" of surrealism.

Gabe's cinematic archive of madness already included *The Cabinet of Dr. Caligari* (1919), the Japanese masterpiece of 1926, *A Page of Madness*, and the global psychoses portrayed in the recent films *A Beautiful Mind* and *Shutter Island*. Perhaps because Gabe was experiencing so many nightmares, he insisted that we stay away from the horror end of the genre (*The Shining*, for example) in favor of films that present madness in a social setting, particularly in the asylum (*Shock Corridor; The Snake Pit; David and Lisa; Girl, Interrupted; Now, Voyager*), and include doctors such as the psychoanalyst, played by Ingrid Bergman, in Hitchcock's *Spellbound*. We placed Peter Robinson's *Asylum*, a documentary of R. D. Laing's anarchist-existentialist experiment with nonhierarchical doctor/patient cohabitation, in tandem with Fredrick Wiseman's *Titicut Follies* (1967), the classic documentary exposé of the horrific conditions of an American mental hospital, the Massachusetts Correctional Institution in Bridgewater. And, of course, Gabe was determined to incorporate the classic films of the antipsychiatry movement into his masterwork. Stanley Kubrick's *A Clockwork Orange* and *One Flew Over the Cuckoo's Nest* became raw material for *Crazy Talk*. Our collaborative work on images from the US War on Terror found its perfect cinematic prophecy in the complicity of psychiatry with torture, behavior modification, and "brainwashing." What Judge Schreber called "soul murder" emerged as an even deeper danger than body counts when the number of military suicides began to surpass US combat deaths.

So Gabe's "*histoire de la folie,*" emulating Godard's nine-hour *Histoire du cinéma,* promised to feature a stream of images, sounds, and texts pillaged from a vast cross-cultural archive, one that would converge on modernity, cinema, and the possibility that madness is a *species* affliction, an even more universal syndrome than Nietzsche's "groups, parties, nations, and epochs." Gabe's "Ship of Fools" would not have been Foucault's place of exile and exclusion but rather the all-inclusive vessel of Spaceship Earth, a precarious updating of Erasmus's *Praise of Folly* leavened by *The Man Who Fell to Earth,* Nicolas Roeg's parable of an alien visitor driven mad by his attempt to understand the human species by watching multiple television programs at the same time.

Crazy Talk previewed the form that the completed work was to have. A hip-hop mash-up of stolen clips and stills from films about madness, *Crazy Talk* is accompanied by a mélange of voices from interviews and performances, and press clippings that document a contemporary epidemic of insanity. Gabe framed all these within cinematic simulations of sensory derangement, the mise en scène of schizophrenia itself, evoking them through special effects and attention to the very nature of the film apparatus and the space of the screen. He ended *Crazy Talk* with two abstract spaces: the first a mathematically ruled grid and the second a vortex in which tiny human figures are whirled, showing the basic dialectic between order and disorder, rationality and madness that he wanted to depict. Not that the meaning of these abstract forms was fixed. In a talk about the film, Gabe noted that the grid could as easily be associated with the prison of grandiosity as with therapeutic rationality and that the vortex reminded him of Blake's symbol of the infinite that resides in a grain of sand: "The nature of Infinity is this: That every thing has its / Own Vortex."

The preproduction "atlas" of the planned film was well on its way toward a reflexive turn toward the very idea of the atlas as such, the crazy attempt to hold up the whole world, to see it all, "as if," in the mad King Lear's moment of imagined lucidity, "we were God's spies." It was to be a Herculean task, foreshadowed by the ambition of the schizophrenic art historian Aby Warburg to create a universal atlas of the *Pathosformel*, the passions and pathologies of human behavior.

I suppose it is clear that, by this point, our fantasies about the film were merging, and his dream was taking over my life as a scholar. Or was it the other way around? Was I swallowing up his project, making it mine? Either way, I am stuck with it, still inside it. Some part of me went over the edge with Gabe and is still falling and flying with him. It was the best part of me. Did it go with him? Into the case—that is, the world—that he created, that he was? I can't let him go and still don't know how to end this book, or if I really want to. It has done little to assuage my guilt for failing him as a father. But neither has it lessened my sense of wonder at the life he gave us. I have never wanted to claim that he was a great undiscovered artist. He was not a Van Gogh, but someone who felt that level of ambition, struck down before he was able to fulfill it. What he gave us was something more profound than an "oeuvre" (Foucault was finally right): it was an idea, a concept of transforming schizophrenia into something useful, putting it to work. Gabe never completed his Infinite Cube, but he did make a model, and Antony Gormley brought it into the world. He never made his nine-hour film or walked on the red carpet at the Academy Awards. But he gave me a model for how to survive and, for a time, prevail over schizophrenia. In the absence of the work, he gave me a job that will never be finished.

Poems by
Janice Misurell-Mitchell

TO GABRIEL FROM MOM, JUNE 27, 2012

How can you be gone
When all around you swirls
The love for you and from you?

How can you be gone
When yet we see your sculptures, drawings
Photos, films and videos
Read your screenplays, hear your songs?

When we see you in our mind's eye
Walking, floppy hat and baggy
Pants and backpack, cigarette

Quiet, staring, thinking
Do we know what you are hearing?
What your mind wants you to follow?
Why it pushes you from all
Who love you, want to love you,
Hold you in their hearts?

You are gone you are gone you are gone — you are you are
YOU ARE

You exist now in another form, a form we make
Of memory, writings, visions, objects

We will not have your humor, your embrace, concern for
    others
Your moods, your anger, your painful accusations
Your beauty, your playfulness, your energies, your joy
Your helpfulness, your growth, your ever-new abilities

You are gone you are gone you are gone
You are
You are with us
You are with us still
You are with us still in silence
In memory
In works
In deeds
In love

We know that you will never see your dreams —
Of spouse and children,

Recognition
Fulfilled

But you have not ended —
As you have said, thoughts travel faster
Than the speed of light
And love can last in depth forever
Although you gave up life,
I cannot give you up
I will not give you up to death
I will not give you up

For me you are not gone
Forever for me you will not be gone
We will try, with all our love,
To make you live
For the rest of our lives

You are not gone, You are not gone
YOU ARE

—*Mama, Mamacita, YoMama, YoYoMama, YoYoMaimonades,
    Momice, Mom*

June 27, 2012

FRIDAY, AUGUST 3, 2012

I understand now how it happened — how the voices got
    louder and louder and more and more

Scrambled and yelling and angry and hating — accusing —

How you heard them
How I see you hear them
How I think I hear them
How I know that's not
        what you heard — yours was worse

But I heard it now and I
Saw it from
Inside and
Out

Like a movie

Like it's real

Like it's all around —

You're on the balcony
Having a smoke
You've been hearing them

And now everything is vibrating
The air, the sounds
Closer and surrounding me —
All the hatred, all the
Words pulsing
Striking
Out at
Me

I escape
Over the railing
I will be free of them
I will be free —

I did not will this
I did not want this
Forgive me

There is nothing to forgive.
I embrace you. Stay with us as you are
We will have to be with you
As you are
Now.

THIS IS NOT A HAIKU

five fucking
miserable months
since suicide Sunday
killing constant creation
dying death destruction
leaving loving life
family

murdered by the voices

November 18, 2012

YOUR BABY'S HERE

Mrs. Mitchell, "Your baby's here."
And there you were
Baby black hair
All wrinkled and squiggly
Curled up, waiting
To be held, loved, nursed

Ehrlichman overhead on TV
Spinning out excuses for Nixon,
The excuse for a president
You were born during political times,
    I thought

Carmen was born during
The Age of Aquarius
And you, the Age of Nixon
The beginning of the
Tangle of Times
Which now has become
The Worst of Times
For us

December 10, 2012

I'M STANDING AT THE FOOT OF THE STAIRS

It's June 22 and I'm
standing at the foot of the
stairs, in the living room
saying "Goodbye", and not knowing
it will be the last time
I see you alive

You've had lunch, coffee
you say you're not feeling well
you're tired
you may not want to go out tonight
(there is the avant-garde opera I'm in,
or a movie with Dad)
I ask you if you'll be all right
you say, "Yes"
I tell you to get some rest
we hug and say "Goodbye"
you go out the door
I watch you go down the street
it was the last time

How not to know
to think it was just another

day, another Friday afternoon
the evening beginning new things
after a week of heady, detailed
music – my *Vanishing Points/Quantum Leaps*
where Pat said you stared at me, conducting,
during the whole piece
and then there was always your
very loud whistle
at all the concerts
when my music was
played, and
you were there.

You did leap
who would have thought

I also ask myself why – why have I always been so
fascinated by voices?

Not just the kids singing in harmony
on the porch
But why the voices in
Metaphorsis?
And I was writing *Mad Song* the winter
you napped upstairs
at Oakland Park

Is it just irony that
you died hearing voices?
what does my attraction to them mean?
and how far can I go with them
and still not threaten?

Poems by Janice Misurell-Mitchell   139

how far can I go without trying
to re-create
what I think
you might have
heard?
and why do I
do this?

I sound like you
when you were
very young
and always asking,
"Why?" until that funny time
in the car
(on a trip to Michigan,
I'm thinking)
you say,
"Why do I ask 'why'?"

Now I just ask "Why?"
when I remember
you

As time goes on
you are farther and farther
away

How to keep you alive
as time goes on
I'm not talking now of
works — we are making that happen
but how to keep you alive

in spirit, in some kind of
presence

I hold your photo,
the one with the great smile
(blue shirt, Columbus)
and I go to the foot of the
stairs

And I remember the last time
I saw you,
hugged you

Stay with us now
In some way
Stay with us.

February 28, 2013

I HAD A HALF DREAM THAT I GOT THERE IN TIME

I had a half dream
on the plane, while
going to
Birmingham
That I got there
in time
I don't remember how
I got in, because
We never could find the keys
on a coiled keychain (green?)
that you gave us.

I still can't find those keys.

So I don't know how I got in, but the scene began with you
on the balcony and me rushing out to get you. You tell
me about the voices getting bad and I tell you to come
inside. You argue, I somehow find out that you lowered
your medication. I somehow get you inside — I think
it's by insisting that you take a 20 mg. pill immediately.
By now your face is red and your head is spinning. There
are attempts to get back outside. I try to pull you back. (I

don't know where Tom is — I think he can't be included because it's my half dream so it's from me about Gabe and me.)

But I do get him to take a pill. He flops on the bed. I am wondering about calling 911 — he doesn't want me to. I can't get into a fight with him. He's not rational, and he can be strong. No physical fights. But then he tries to get up, and I try to stop him. This is very difficult. I think about calling 911 psychiatric — would they be okay? — or trying to get him to Northwestern Memorial — but Emergency could be awful, and I don't think they'd give him a sedative right away — but actually maybe they would — if he would be getting psychotic.

I thought about after — hospital bed, coming down to the house. Could he ever live in the condo again? How could we prevent him from jumping? Even if he had more medication, it might not have prevented it.

I didn't know they could drive him to it. And I do believe it was a momentary thing — not to diminish its power — it's just that it was a confluence of circumstances, all going the wrong way.

Why this all came to me on the plane — I felt I was basically awake. But this story and these images seemed to insist on being there. And I was actively involved in it, so it was sort of a waking dream. I think it's something I needed to work out. I don't think it's over, but I do think I got somewhere with it. These days it's possible for me to visualize him with his hair down and with glasses.

For quite a while I found a younger face to look at, one without glasses. Except for that one night when I saw his face, hair spread, against a background of red. It felt like a vision.

Anyway, now I can see him in a wider variety of stages. And that's good. My difficulty is that I can only dwell on the past, while I really want to make new memories, with him in them. The film is one way, but I am also trying others.

February 26, 2014

CHICAGO, JUNE 24, 2014, 9:30PM, CA

Two years
We have lit candles in our various places
Sometimes sung, meditated
Carmen in LA, Tom in Beijing, Janice in Chicago —
Chloe comes barreling into the kitchen
One of your pen and inks
From the group of four
Falls to the floor
Eight inches away
From the wall
It does not break
I scream, shout, cry
Sit on the couch
Perhaps as I did
Two years earlier

But this time
You are there.

BROOKLYN, JULY 23, 2014

Florence talks about you and
Her large plant, root-bound and dry
Flops over at the sound of your name.

THE B TRAIN, JULY 25, 2014 (YOUR BIRTHDAY)

I see everyone on the train
Through your eyes
With kindness
And appreciation
For each person

BEACH HOUSE IN BELMAR, JULY 28, 2014

We're here
You're here
In our minds
In our hearts
Little Elan
Sweet Sophia
Dancing and playing
Instruments of all sorts
To the music
of the "Groanups"
I ache that you are not here
But I hold Elan
As he strums guitar strings
And bangs on drums
And all flat surfaces
And makes sounds of joy
Can you feel this?

THANKSGIVING 2014

thanksgiving thanks
giving thanks for
you
our life with you
now lost
and found, in
memory and in
pain of loss

I think
of giving
to you
and forgiving
you
for giving
me such
deep and lasting
sadness

your way
of giving
made people feel
blessed

and confused about
who you were

who you were —
some of this
you kept from us
you had that right
an obligation, you thought,
not to hurt
further
to protect us

but it didn't work
we should have known
we sat there,
self-enclosed, blinded,
not seeing, or knowing
what was there
that harmed you
and took from you
your life

ANTONY AND GABRIEL: A CHRONICLE OF THE
INFINITE CUBE

London, July, 2007
Antony, always curious
   questioning
   appreciative of
Young artists, sees
Gabe's *Desolation Row Revisited*
"Play that again! Remarkable!
   Yes!"

Chicago, November, 2010
Early evening
Post-lecture
Dark, cold, windy
Northerly Island
I drive Antony and Gabe
   to the bike path there
Light jackets, no hats
They hurry to the center of the lawn
"And this is where your
Iron man should go,
So when the sun rises,

he'll be coming
out of the Lake
through the trees
and out to the lawn."
"Yes! Yes!"

2011
Gabe thinks about
cubes — how they
encompass, letting in
light, lawn, skies,
and protect, he thinks
later, from the vortex —
the swirling unknown
"Or is that grandiosity?"
he asks, slyly

2013
Antony thinks about
Gabe's plan – the Infinite Cube
and tells us, "Yes! I can create that!"

2015
Inside the Infinite Cube
the parallel lines curve
perhaps to meet
The circle may be squared
as *pi* travels on to Infinity
Where lines meet
and cross into an
Infinite future

Where there are no longer
accusing voices
Where one's mind and soul
can be free.

January 28–February 10, 2015

THE INFINITE CUBE

a thousand lights lined
shining in rows infinite
thus our son survives

June 30, 2015, Berlin

WE'LL NEVER KNOW

We'll never know
What you heard
Before you plunged
To your death

The demons got
Too strong
Screaming at you
From within

Your strength
Which had borne you
Through eighteen years
Of pain and beauty
Could no longer keep you
Away and separate from them

The searing pain and turmoil
A moment of insanity
Drove you

To leave the world you loved so much
To leave the world that loved you
So much

I will try to think of you
In your relentless fight
Against them
That the beautiful person you were
Flowered in spite of them
Grew in spite of them
And loved each one of us
In spite of them

June 28, 2017

Gabriel's Email to the Family, on Grammy's Death

It is with Grammy's best gift of persistence and will to live that I too will share these words with you: "If I should lose faith in my darkest hour, my hopes shall be diminished." We all must follow Grammy's example, and we all do in our own way, and as I said in my eulogy—there is a faster speed than the speed of light, the speed of thought. . . . That's what Grampa Rocco would tell you, our memories are what keep them alive in the world, and our hopes are what will eventually reunite us with them. Do not hesitate to love each other fully, to teach the generations to come. . . . Grammy's recipes were more than just good food, they were and are windows into a deep tradition, when she gave us food she was giving us life. She gave us a road map for our emotions. And in every meal she made she was giving us an initiation into the tribe, a rite of passage.

Charles Darwin rightly termed this passage as: "An egress

toward perfection" in which each generation must not only evolve, but improve upon the previous one. How will we advance the cause of Grammy and Grampa? Each of us must choose a most personal path, for each of us there is a recipe, or a theory, or emotion, or poem, or career. As I tell my old friends at the grocery store: "There ain't no goodbyes on this job, only long hellos." Grammy always said hello to Grampa at sunrise, and goodbye at sunset—and I'll see you tomorrow Rocco. Nobody knows how long eternity is, but the Universe is a place as big as we imagine it to be. And we must think of today, and we should save our hellos and goodbyes, and our love for those people who share life with us. Grammy and Grandpa will have us too, and we will have them, and everyone will dance and sing, and eat. . . . Eternity is a long time, but memories can pass through time and space faster than anything, no rocket ship or time machine can take you where you want to be faster than the simple memory of a meal, maybe it was chicken with breadcrumbs, I can smell it, taste it, and remember it in all its perfection. I hope to one day pass Grammy and Grampa on to generations yet to come. I love you all because that is how I was raised, and each of us takes this message forward in time and space. Goodbye is only until the sun rises again.

Lovingly, Gabriel
Oct. 5, 2009

ACKNOWLEDGMENTS

A book like this does not get written alone. It is difficult to break the habits of a scholar who believes (against all evidence) that the answer to every question is to be found somewhere in a book, or in wise, learned colleagues. Therefore, this memoir is not just memory but also critical reflection, complete with references to secondary sources, second guessing ("would have, should have, could have"), and the undefeated wish to be telling a different story altogether, one in which Gabe would have survived schizophrenia, gone on to fame and fortune, and become the caregiver for his aging dad. Every history implies alternate histories, every memoir, counter-memories.

A memoir also turns out to be a collaborative effort of recall, in which dates, details, and events slowly come into focus within a kaleidoscope of scenes and conversations. In this work, I have enjoyed the steadfast support of those closest to Gabe, starting with his mother and my spouse of fifty years, Janice Misurell-Mitchell (who corrected my inaccurate dates, reminded me of what was actually said, and contributed her poems to this book). Janice also made Gabe's life possible, both his twenty-year survival and flourishing as an artist and person, and this story of his life. Gabe's sister, Carmen Elena Mitchell, was his muse and confidant, and her film *Infinite Light* promises to bring him to life in the medium he was attempting to master. So this is really a family memoir, with Gabe at its center, and myself as the scribe.

I have lost track of how many times this memoir has been rewritten, largely due to amazingly perceptive readings by friends and colleagues. Bill Ayers read the first draft, indeed the very first words I wrote in the days immediately after Gabe's death, as he bustled around feeding and caring for my grief-stricken family. Rachel DeWoskin read the penultimate draft as if it were a puzzle that had been scattered on a table and rearranged the pieces for me to make the whole picture snap into view. In between the first and last drafts, Elizabeth Abel, Carol J. Adams, Lauren Berlant, Charles Bernstein, Jonathan Bordo, Ellen Esrock, Jonathan Lear, Svi Lothane, Louis Sass, and Florence Tager provided readings that corrected my course and urged me to plunge ahead.

In his lifetime, those who encouraged Gabe to do something worthy of a memoir included Antony Gormley, Henry Louis Gates Jr., Julia Kristeva, Marie-José Mondzain, Marguerite and Jacques Derrida, Homi Bhabha, and Norman MacLeod; those who taught him how to think with cinema, Jim Chandler, Judy Hoffman, Tom Gunning, Miriam Hansen, Yuri Tsivian, and Michael Wilmington.

Those who Gabe recruited for his Superhero Film Society: Hillary Chute and Patrick Jagoda.

The inspiration for his film entitled *Grid Theory*: Hannah Higgins.

My coteachers in the first seminar on this topic, "Seeing Madness," University of Chicago, Winter term, 2011: Françoise Meltzer and Bernard Rubin.

My faithful editor, first reader, and *consigliere*: Alan Thomas.

My research assistants: Rivky Mondal, Jean-Thomas Tremblay.

The staff of *Critical Inquiry*, Hank Scotch and Hannah Christensen.

His last best friend: Danny Russell, the Mayor of Marina City. His forever best friend, Alex Freund. The person he loved, Cricket Leigh.

The therapists and social workers who helped Gabe survive schizophrenia for almost twenty years: Joe Kerouac, Andre Nickerson, Heidi Tansley, Jill Voronoff, Dan Blankenberger, Marcia Brontman, and Will Cronenwett.

Gabe's grandparents: Rocco and Florence Misurell, Leona Gaertner Mitchell Maupin, and the ghost of my father, "Grandpa Tom" Mitchell.

Those who were part of Gabe's story: Bernardine Dohrn and Bill Ayers, Shlomo Sher, Michael-Rocco Misurell, Justin Misurell, Carrick Bell, Robert Misurell ("Uncle Mizzie"), Patti Villastrego ("Aunt Patti"), Stephanie Lighte, Regina Hunter, Lauren Hunter, Adam Day, Daniel Pettigrew, Pat Mullen, Roseanne Rini, Bonita Plymale, Sandra and Mike Ryan ("Aunt Sandra and Uncle Mike"), Stephanie and Gordon Medlock, Alanna Medlock, Randy Albers, Nan and Evan Freund, Rob Friedman and Mindy Hutchison, Blair Barbour, Becky and Jim Chandler, Tanya Fernando, Patricia and Philip Morehead, Bob Johnson, Mara Fortes, Zoey Schmolowitz, and Zayd Dohrn.

NAMI, and Thresholds: Dennis Hills-Cooper.

Contributors, whether they know it or not, to the post-production phase of this book: Arild Fetveit, Jeremy Gilbert-Rolfe, Peter Goodrich, Richard Neer, Robert Pippin, Peter Schwartz, Vanessa Schwartz, Joel Snyder, Yuri Tsivian, Georges Didi-Huberman, Hilde van Gelder, Mieke Bal, and Justin Underhill. The students in my seminars: "Seeing Madness," Winter 2011; "Movies and Madness," Spring, 2013; "Reading Madness," Fall, 2015.

FURTHER READING & VIEWING

EPIGRAPH

"The Mental Traveller," the poem by William Blake that provides the title for this book, was never published in his lifetime. It is included in a handwritten collection of ten poems that Blake made around 1803 for a friend or patron. It is now known as "The Pickering Manuscript" after its appearance in the collection B. M. Pickering in 1866. See David Erdman, *The Poetry and Prose of William Blake* (Garden City, NY: Doubleday, 1979), 475–77, and 776–77.

PREFACE

The distinction between books that I have wanted to write, as opposed to the ones (like this) that I had to write, is of course deeply problematic, given the strong relationship between publishing and perishing in academia. Nevertheless, writing for me has always been high on a list that includes drinking a fine whiskey and breathing. For a more complete bibliography, see my home page: https://lucian.uchicago.edu/blogs/wjtmitchell/.

While I do not subscribe to R. D. Laing's militancy as a leading figure in the antipsychiatry movement, I do take seriously his intimate and sympathetic engagements with schizophrenia, which have been part of my own formation since the 1960s. On the analogy between schizophrenia and the "broken heart," see *The Politics of Experience* (New York: Pantheon Books, 1967), 129. See also Louis Sass's reflections on the naming of schizophrenia as illness or identity, "'Schizophrenic Person' or 'Person with Schizophrenia'? An Essay on Illness and the Self," *Theory and Psychology* 17(3): 395–420. Angela Woods' *The Sublime Object of Psychiatry: Schizophrenia in Clinical and Cultural Theory* (Oxford University Press, 2011) provides an excellent critical survey of the antipsychiatry movement and the role of the term "schizophrenia" as a "sublime" and indefinable category in modern discourses about mental illness. See also Michael Staub's *Madness Is Civilization* (Chicago: University of Chicago Press, 2011), a discussion of mental illness in the framework of social theory. E. Fuller Torrey's *Surviving Schizophrenia: A Manual for Families, Consumers, and Providers* (New York: Harper Collins, 1983) served as a kind of family bible, along with the DSM (*Diagnostic and Statistical Manual of Mental Disorders*) over the course of Gabriel's illness.

CHAPTER 1

Crazy Talk, along with Gabriel's other films, is available on YouTube, accessible by way of his website, *Philmworx.com*.

Jean-Luc Godard's *Histoire du cinéma* is a nine-hour video project initiated in the late 1980s and completed in 1998. Alefeleti Brown remarks in *Senses of Cinema* (March 2008), "Surely, the mastery of *Histoire(s)* ebbs from Godard's particular status in the cinema, his tireless devotion and aptitude for quotation and connection—as if he is the sole channel through which the madness and chaos of so much ephemera finds any bearing." This precisely matches Gabe's cinematic sensibility and is what inspired his *Histoire de la folie*. The special relationship between movies and madness has been a founding insight of cinema studies since the beginnings of the medium. Jean-Luis Baudry seems to collapse cinema, dream, and psychosis into a single phenomenon: "Cinema offers an artificial psychosis without offering the dreamer the possibility of exercising any kind of immediate control." "The Apparatus: Metapsychological Approaches to the Impression of Reality in the Cinema," in *Narrative, Apparatus, Ideology: A Film Theory Reader*, ed. Philip Rosen (New York: Columbia University Press, 1986), 299–318.

The stigma of schizophrenia was, in Gabe's view, even worse than the actual symptoms, a claim that one finds echoed in the observation of E. Fuller Torrey that "people with schizophrenia are the lepers of the present day." *Surviving Schizophrenia*, 8.

Michel Foucault, "Madness, the Absence of an Oeuvre," in *History of Madness* (New York: Routledge, 2006), 541–49.

Many of Janice's compositions and performances can be found on her website: https://jmisurell-mitchell.com/.

Patrick B. Mullen pioneered folklore studies at Ohio State from the 1970s onward. An annual prize for the best essay in folklore is named after him.

The New University Conference was a national organization of radical graduate students, staff, and faculty that opened a chapter on the University of Chicago campus in the spring of 1968. The group was intended to serve as a collective organizing body to support and promote the entire range of contemporaneous leftist movements. The Ohio State University chapter was founded in the living room of Florence Tager, a graduate student in history at OSU in 1969, our second year in Columbus.

For further information about Rocco Misurell's career as a high school principal, see Ben Horowitz, *Newark School Gives Hope to Dropouts*, *New York Times*, July 2, 1978, https://www.nytimes.com/1978/07/02/archives/new-jersey-weekly-newark-school-gives-hope-to-dropouts.html.

CHAPTER 2

Mad Magazine moved to 485 MADison Avenue in the early 1960s. It is now located in Los Angeles. During the week I wrote these words, the demise of the magazine was announced.

A special issue of *Critical Inquiry*, "Comics & Media," edited by Hillary Chute and Patrick Jagoda, was published in the spring of 2014 (vol. 40, no. 3) and includes my interviews with Art Spiegelman and Joe Sacco. My afterword to this issue includes an extensive discussion of Nathaniel McClennen's graphic "thank-you note."

The idea that identity is a product of an endangered sense of self and belonging I owe to anthropologist Glenn Bowman, "The Exilic Imagination," in *The Landscape of Palestine: Equivocal Poetry* (Birzeit University Publications, 1999), 57.

CHAPTER 3

Thought disorder is a catch-all term that forms one of the foundational binary oppositions of psychiatry between disorders of emotion ("mood disorders") and ideas or thoughts. Bipolar or "manic depressive" illnesses are generally classified as mood disorders, while schizophrenia is associated with delusional thinking, paranoia, and hallucinatory experiences such as voices and visions. Our experience was that these neat divisions routinely collapsed, and that the boundary between Gabriel's thoughts and feelings was very porous. Nevertheless, I have talked to highly qualified psychiatrists since his death who pronounce, with utter confidence, that he must have been bipolar. Needless to say, these pronouncements strike me as unprofessional at best and, at worst, pure bullshit.

Derrida was a frequent visitor to the University of Chicago from the 1980s until his death in 2004. I met him first in 1968 when I was a star-struck graduate student at Johns Hopkins University when he came for the famous "Structuralist Symposium." Later, as editor of *Critical Inquiry*, I frequently hosted him for lectures and published many of his key essays: on apartheid as "Racism's Last Word," his famous defense of Paul de Man, "Biodegradables," "The Gift," and "The Law of Genre." My essays on his work include "Dead Again," a preface to *The Late Derrida*, which I coedited in book form with Arnold Davidson (Chicago: University of Chicago Press, 2007), and "Picturing Terror: Derrida's Autoimmunity" *Critical Inquiry* 33, no. 2 (Spring 2007): 277–290.

CHAPTER 4

The idea that the human brain "emits thirty times as much energy as an equivalent volume of the sun" was suggested to me by Ren Weschler. I have no idea if it is true, but it certainly felt that way in the winter of 1994 during Gabe's first real psychotic episode. Daniel Paul Schreber's *Memoir of My Nervous Illness* (1903) became the most famous first-person account of schizophrenia in the twentieth century, first immortalized by Freud's treatment of it in *The Schreber Case* (1911). It has become the central text in a voluminous literature and has spurred endless controversies over the causes of Schreber's illness (domineering father, bad doctors, mistreatment and involuntary confinement). Among the many books on the topic, I have found Eric Santner's *My Own Private Germany* (Princeton, NJ: Princeton University Press, 1998), which places it in a sociopolitical context, and Henry Zvi Lothane's *In Defense of Schreber* (London: Analytic Press, 1989), especially useful.

The image of the human body emanating "nervous fibres" appears in the work of William Blake and in the work of schizophrenic artists like Jakob Mohr in the University of Heidelberg's Prinzhorn Collection.

Freud's concept of transference involves the bonding of the analysand with the analyst, in which something like parental trust and love is transferred to the analyst. Of course, the transference can also take negative forms of resentment, anger, and hatred.

Social Security Disability Insurance, or SSDI, pays a monthly benefit to those who qualify. The benefit amount is based on your age and the amount you've paid into Social Security while working. According to the National Alliance on Mental Illness, the average SSDI benefit was $900 per month in 2009. Given that the national median rent, per the Census Bureau, was $842 that year, SSDI isn't enough to cover rent and other expenses like food and prescriptions. The US Department of Housing and Urban Development, or HUD, helps to ease the burden of high housing costs by providing funds for housing assistance through Housing Choice Vouchers, formerly known as Section 8.

CHAPTER 5

Chicago's remarkable Thresholds agency (http://www .thresholds.org/) provides social services and medical advice for young people struggling with mental illness. It has a variety of programs, including housing, job training, educational opportunities, art therapy, and social work supervision. I regard it as the key factor in Gabe's ability to survive schizophrenia for almost twenty years and to have something like a real life, with meaningful work and lasting friendships.

Plato's concept of "initiatory madness," exemplified by the Bacchanalian festival, is discussed in *The Phaedrus*, along with his notions of poetic, prophetic, and amatory madness.

Zyprexa (olanzapine) is an antipsychotic medication that affects chemicals in the brain. Zyprexa is used to treat the symptoms of psychotic conditions such as schizophrenia and bipolar disorder (manic depression) in adults and children who are at least thirteen years old.

CHAPTER 6

There is no way to overstate the importance of our friendship with Bill Ayers and Bernardine Dohrn during and after Gabe's life. We had seen up close how they kept their parents close to them, moving them into their home after they had fallen into dementia and Alzheimer's. Bernardine was in Amsterdam during the week after Gabe's death, or she surely would have been there with us as well. Bill was also the first person (after Janice) to read this memoir. Gabe's last film was a mash-up of images from 1968 accompanied by a voice-over of Bill reading from his memoir, *Fugitive Days*.

Gabe's frequent references to the suicidal leap in the film *Vanilla Sky* include the implication that the hero's death in the illusory world of a cryogenic incubator will turn out to be an awakening into reality. The title of the Spanish film on which *Vanilla Sky* is based is *Abre Los Ojos* ("Open Your Eyes"). Suicide is a fatal convergence of the "fight or flight" impulse—a combination of aggression against and escape from the self. Gabe's self-portrait as somnambulist portrays his own death as a fall and a flight from (and fight against) the lucid nightmares of schizophrenia.

CHAPTER 7

If you want to see for yourself the Masada lesson of collective suicide, I recommend Avi Moghrabi's film, *Avenge but One of My Two Eyes* (2005), where it is recited by the tour guide and then firmly criticized by a young American Jewish woman, who points out that suicide is forbidden by Jewish law.

Wigger: "A male caucasian, usually born and raised in the suburbs that displays a strong desire to emulate African American Hip Hop culture and style through 'Bling' fashion and generally accepted 'thug life'" guiding principles" (https://www.urbandictionary.com/define.php?term=wigger).

CHAPTER 8

I hope it will not spoil the game to give you the answers left out of the main text: *The Treasure of the Sierra Madre* (John Huston, 1948) and *Sunset Boulevard* (Billy Wilder, 1950).

"Mad Pride is a mass movement of the users of services, former users, and the aligned," which argues "individuals with mental illness should be proud of their 'mad' identity. It was formed in 1993 in response to local community prejudices toward people with a psychiatric history living in boarding homes in the Parkdale area of Canada, and an event has been held every year since then in the city except for 1996. A similar movement began around the same time in the United Kingdom. By the late 1990s similar events were being organized under the Mad Pride name around the globe. . . . Events draw thousands of participants, according to a United States mental health advocacy organization that promotes and tracks events spawned by the movement." https://en.wikipedia.org /wiki/Mad_Pride.

The late Prashant Barghava (1973–2015) had been Gabriel's friend since high school, part of the graffiti boys at Kenwood Academy. He was a successful filmmaker whose feature length film, *Patang: The Kite* was premiered to great acclaim at the Berlin International Film Festival and the Tribeca Film Festival in 2012. He encouraged Gabe's ambitions as a filmmaker, corresponding with him about his script for *Da Jewels*. In the weeks after Gabe's death, he arranged to have *Crazy Talk* shown at the Chicago premiere of *Patang*. Sadly, Prashant only outlived Gabe by three years, dying of a heart attack in 2015.

"Open your eyes" are the last words of the film and the title of the Spanish language film, *Abre Los Ojos* (Alejandro Amenabar, 1997) on which *Vanilla Sky* (Cameron Crowe, 2001) is based.

CHAPTER 9

A Beautiful Mind (Ron Howard, 2001), portrays John Nash's overcoming of schizophrenia as a simple matter of will power, a conscious decision to ignore his hallucinations and tell them to go away. It is hard to imagine a more implausible portrayal of how to deal with the symptoms of schizophrenia. One of the many virtues of Elyn Saks's autobiography, *The Center Cannot Hold*, is its clear-eyed recognition that the management of schizophrenia involves an acceptance that it is incurable, and a recognition that will power is not enough.

A good basic account of Aby Warburg's struggle with schizophrenia is provided by Ernst Gombrich, *Aby Warburg: An Intellectual Biography* (London: The Warburg Institute, 1970). Elyn Saks's memoir, *The Center Cannot Hold* (New

York: Hachette, 2008), describes numerous suicide attempts and hospitalizations, a pattern that seems typical. Gabe was unusual in having only one hospitalization and one suicide attempt.

CHAPTER 10

Louis Sass's discussion of this basic paradox of "sovereign servitude" in schizophrenia is the best account of this that I know. See *The Paradoxes of Delusion: Wittgenstein, Schreber, and the Schizophrenic Mind* (Ithaca, NY: Cornell University Press, 1994).

For Freud's account of false memories that seem true, see his essay, "Screen Memories" (1899), in *Standard Edition* (London: Hogarth Press), vol. 3, 301–22.

The Duck-Rabbit was a constant obsession in my own writing from the early 1990s. It is what Gestalt psychology calls a "multistable image," and can be seen as a duck one minute, a rabbit the next. See my essay "Metapictures" in *Picture Theory* (Chicago: University of Chicago Press, 1994).

CHAPTER 11

A large number of mentally ill people are now making their condition public on social media, especially YouTube. Rachel Star is a schizophrenic who offers advice to people who have the illness, or who are interacting with a schizophrenic. See https://psychcentral.com/blog/inside-schizophrenia-what-is-schizophrenia/. See also "Talking about My Schizophrenia," by MortenErCrazy, https://www.youtube.com/watch?v=B1YvJWTWWEk.

See above for the discussion of the literature on Schreber.

E. Fuller Torrey discusses the prevalence of chain-smoking in individuals with schizophrenia as a form of self-medication. *Surviving Schizophrenia*, 4th ed. (New York: Harper Collins, 2001), 277.

The title of Eric Santner's *My Own Private Germany*, about the historical and media context of Schreber's schizophrenia, echoes the title of the film, *My Own Private Idaho* (Gus Van Sant, 1991). Gabe and I devoured this film, with its amazing treatment of addiction, and its stunning appearance by William Burroughs, playing himself.

The image of the Hooded Man of Abu Ghraib became a central theme, and the cover art, for my book *Cloning Terror: The War of Images, 9-11 to the Present* (Chicago: University of Chicago Press, 2011).

Ray Kurzweil, *The Singularity Is Near* (New York: Penguin, 2006).

See Fred Turner, *From Counterculture to Cyberculture* (Chicago: University of Chicago Press, 2006), for a detailed examination of the way that the utopian intellectuals of "my" era (the Sixties) laid the groundwork for Gabriel's.

Marshall McLuhan, *Understanding Media: The Extensions of Man*, famously declared that the invention of electricity had enabled the extension of the central nervous system in unprecedented forms of global communication networks.

Grid Theory drew its images from Hannah Higgins, *The Grid Book* (Cambridge, MA: MIT Press, 2009). Hannah is my former student and a lifelong friend. She is also the daughter of the Fluxus founder, Dick Higgins; through her, Gabe learned a thing or two about Fluxus performances.

CHAPTER 12

The title of this chapter echoes Erving Goffman's classic essay "The Moral Career of the Mental Patient" in his book *Asylums:*

Essays on the Social Situation of Mental Patients and Other Inmates (New York: Anchor Books, 1961).

"Guardianship" is the most difficult and power-laden role the caregiver can face. This was mainly Janice's role in handling his allowance, bills, and Social Security benefits. Seventy-seven percent of caregivers of adult children report that "a healthcare provider or professional was unable to speak to them." NAC report, op. cit., 28.

See Fuller Torrey, *Surviving Schizophrenia*, 114, on the Kennedy family's long ordeal with Rosemary (John, Robert, and Edward Kennedy's sister). After a childhood of mental retardation, she displayed psychotic symptoms at age twenty-one and was subjected to a lobotomy that left her with severe brain damage.

For a preview of Carmen Mitchell's biopic about Gabriel's struggle with schizophrenia, see her short film, *Infinite Light*, https://www.youtube.com/watch?v=GGqty3BFd9Q.

The most alarming statistic is that 60 percent of male schizophrenics will attempt suicide; about 5–10 percent succeed. Their rate of "success" is significantly higher than that of women, *schizophrenia.com/suicide.html*.

I am indebted here to the work of Carol J. Adams on the role of the caregivers with aging parents suffering from dementia. See her essay "Toward a Philosophy of Care," *Critical Inquiry* 43, no. 4 (Summer 2017), 765–89.

CHAPTER 13

The question of the "case" was posed by my longtime colleague, Lauren Berlant, who had edited a pair of special issues of *Critical Inquiry* (33:4 [Summer 2007], and 36:4 [Summer 2010]) entitled "On the Case." My sense of the meaning of cases and case histories is largely informed by the essays in this issue, which range over sociology, law, medicine, state taxonomies, and aesthetic genres.

"The world is all that is the case" is Ludwig Wittgenstein's opening postulate in his *Tractatus Logico-Philosophicus* (1921). He follows it, significantly, by asserting that "the world is the totality of facts, not of things," and facts (as opposed to things) exist in "logical space." The world, in short, is a factitious entity, artificially created. This is usually taken to mean that it is fake or counterfeit, but that does not prevent it from becoming a practical reality. Was Gabriel's illness, insofar as it constructed a world of delusion and fantasy and was in turn constructed by the terms of psychiatry, all there was to his case? My sense is that things were never quite that simple. The case exceeds the logical space that defines a world; it is full of things beyond "the facts" that are not dreamt of in philosophy. In *The Paradoxes of Delusion: Wittgenstein, Schreber, and the Schizophrenic Mind* (Ithaca, NY: Cornell University Press, 1994), Louis Sass argues that Schreber was a solipsist, inhabiting a paradoxical world in which the subject is an "enslaved sovereign," whose thinking is both omnipotent and impotent at the same time. Certainly there is some of this in Gabriel's self-images of grandiosity, as in his script for *American Dreamers*. The question is whether the logical arguments against solipsism confuse the victory of logic with the efficacy of therapy. Is it enough to constantly win arguments against a schizophrenic mentality as if it were a philosophical position that could be overcome? Or is this more like crashing through an open door? Proving, for instance, that Judge Schreber constantly contradicts himself does not seem like much of a breakthrough, and it treats Schreber completely out of context, with no recognition of his legal profession, his struggles with the laws of "tutelage" or involuntary confinement, and the contemporary antipsychiatry movement. Was Wittgenstein's own struggle with madness, which Sass describes so well, cured by philosophy?

Leonard Cohen, "Anthem." The great Canadian troubadour was another passion that I shared with Gabriel, who memorized along with me the lyrics of "Suzanne," "Hallelujah," "Sisters of Mercy," and "Marianne" and puzzled over the meaning of the lines "First we'll take Manhattan / Then we'll take Berlin."

Gabriel attended Derrida's Carpenter lectures on the gift at the University of Chicago in 1990 and was able to meet with the great philosopher at our home in Chicago and in Paris. He was well aware of the double-edged significance of gifts and giftedness. Derrida's lecture "Given Time: The Time of the King" appeared in *Critical Inquiry* 18:2 (Winter 1992), 161–87.

Sander Gilman, *Seeing the Insane* (Lincoln, Nebraska: University of Nebraska Press, 1982) is the best general introduction to the portrayal of madness in Western art and visual culture.

A course description and syllabus for "Seeing Madness" is available on my home page, https://lucian.uchicago.edu/blogs/wjtmitchell/courses/.